Vietnamese

B I B L E

Vietnamese
BIBLE

Jacki Passmore

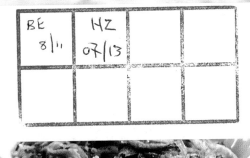

Contents

Introduction

Vietnamese cuisine has so many influences – Chinese woks and chopsticks, French crème caramel and crisp baguettes, and Thai-style flavours are all present. Yet its personality and style is uniquely Vietnamese, characterised by an abundance of fresh herbs, crisp lettuce, noodles and soft rice-paper wraps. And served with almost everything are fragrant and tangy dipping sauces, roasted peanuts, fried shallots and garlic.

Vietnamese food can be served as several courses together, or presented as a western-style three-course meal, beginning with soup or an appetiser, followed by one or two noodle or rice dishes, and fresh fruit or something sweet to finish.

Big bowls of soupy noodles are a meal in themselves and a snack at any time of the day. For drinks there are iced beverages and white wine, or Chinese-style green or black tea (*che* or *tra*) served before or after the meal.

Vietnamese Basics

Vietnam has a vast network of rivers, streams, ponds and canals, which provide plentiful water-transport and farming opportunities in the delta regions, while cool-climate vegetables and herbs proliferate at higher elevations.

Preparing a Vietnamese meal is easy to do. Cooking and preparation techniques are clearly explained, as are details for setting up your kitchen with the ingredients you will require. There are recipes for tasty, tangy, dipping sauces and other basics needed to make delicious Vietnamese food. Adjust the amounts of the four key seasonings (fish sauce, sugar, chilli and lime juice) to suit your individual taste.

Vietnamese Coffee

The French brought their coffee habit to Vietnam in the 1800's; a leisurely affair brewed at the table through a small metal filter which fits over the coffee cup. Boiling water slowly drips through the ground coffee to make a dark brew taken black (*ca phe*) or sweetened with condensed milk (*ca phe sua*).

The Kitchen

The Vietnamese kitchen is basic, with a small, moulded clay cooker fired with wood chips for wok cooking, and with glowing charcoal for grilling and slow simmering. You can cook on a regular stove, a wok ring attached to a barbecue, or on a small portable gas-fired cooker set on a table top.

Keep your wok in perfect condition for stir-frying by scrubbing with a soft brush after use, and rubbing the interior with paper towel dipped in oil to bring on a lustrous glaze. A flat-edged wok spatula and a wire skimmer, or slotted spoon, are wok companions you can't do without. And if your wok doesn't fit snugly over your cook top, purchase a metal wok-frame to hold it steady.

For rice cooking, use a saucepan with a heavy base and a well-fitted lid. Sticky rice can be cooked in a steamer over a saucepan.

For steaming, simply use a bamboo steamer over a wok or saucepan, or you might want to purchase a tiered Asian steamer at low cost from Asian food and kitchen supply stores.

A cast-iron hot plate over a gas ring, a hibachi barbecue, or a basic gas- or charcoal-fired barbecue will take care of grilling needs. Remember to clean after use and rub down with an oiled cloth to maintain a good non-stick cooking surface.

No Vietnamese cook can operate without a stone mortar in which to grind herbs and spices, and crush seasonings and salad ingredients. Their preference is for a large wooden pestle, but a stone pestle is fine. A clean electric coffee grinder is easier to use, and is preferable to a blender or food processor for grinding small quantities of herbs and spices.

For thinly sliced grilled meat and fragile seafood, check out camping stores for an inexpensive hinged wire-toaster. Its two looped wire handles lock together making for easy turning.

A Chinese cleaver is the best utensil for chopping straight through bones when preparing poultry, and with a bit of practice it can become an indispensible knife for most kitchen chores.

Any large, deep saucepan can be used for soup stock. For table-top cooking, use a fondu set, an electric frypan, or a saucepan, wok or frying pan over a portable gas cooker. Small portable induction cookers have recently come onto the market. They are inexpensive to buy and operate, and perfect for cooking on the table or outdoors.

The Pantry

Keeping the pantry stocked with the basics needed for Vietnamese cooking is convenient and inexpensive. Ingredients such as canned bamboo shoots, coconut milk or cream, dried shrimp in a jar, fish sauce, bamboo skewers and flours for coating and thickening,

like cornflour, will cater to most recipe requirements. Noodles, rice sticks and rice vermicelli, egg or bean-thread noodles are also commonly used. For more information see Special Ingredients on page 248.

The Garden

Plant soft-leaf coriander, saw-leaf coriander, perilla, basil, dill, Vietnamese mint, chillies, lemongrass, spring onions and garlic chives to supply your kitchen needs.

Food Preparation

SEAFOOD

Shell **prawns** and press top ends and tails together to force the body into a curved shape. Insert the point of a bamboo skewer or toothpick into the top of the curve about 3 mm (⅛ in) below the surface, and slowly ease the pick upwards. It will break the flesh, and draw the grit-filled dark vein to the surface, where it can be gently eased out.

With a sharp knife, cut deeply along the centre back of the prawn for its full length. Press out flat to make butterflied prawn cutlets.

To clean **squid**, grasp head, twist and bring the intestines with it. Reach a finger into the tube, loosen the transparent quill and remove. Rinse squid and drain.

For recipes that require 'pineapple cut' squid, Cut the squid open along one side, open out flat with the inner surface facing up. With a sharp knife scrape off any soft tissue, and then score the squid in a crosshatch of deep cuts about 1 cm (⅜ in) apart, taking care not to cut through. This tenderises and gives the squid an attractive 'pineapple skin' effect when cooked. Cut into 3-cm (1¼ in) squares.

CHILLIES

When working with chillies, wear latex gloves, or wash hands thoroughly with soapy water after. Be careful never to rub your eyes after touching chillies.

To deseed chillies, slit open and scrape out seeds and pale filaments with the tip of your knife.

SOFTENING DRIED RICE PAPERS (BANH TRANG) & RICE VERMICELLI

Have a bowl of lukewarm water ready and a clean cloth. Turn the dried papers in the water one at a time for 20–30 seconds or until they become slightly limp. Lift out and spread on a cloth. They will continue to soften. When ready they should be pliable, but dry to touch. When over-softened, they tear easily.

Place dried rice vermicelli in a bowl and cover with boiling water. Let sit for 3–4 minutes until they turn white and soft. Tip into a colander to drain, and then snip into 8 cm (3 in) lengths using kitchen scissors. Keep soft by sprinkling on a few drops of peanut or sesame oil and running fingers through the noodles to evenly coat them. Cover with cling wrap and refrigerate until needed.

ROASTING PEANUTS

Spread raw shelled peanuts on an oven tray and roast at 180°C (360°F) for about 10 minutes, or until the skins loosen. Tip into a clean kitchen cloth and rub to remove skins. Return skinned peanuts to the oven for a few more minutes until lightly golden brown. Do not over-cook as they continue to brown for a few minutes out of the oven. When cool, chop or crush as required.

Appetisers

In every town, city, beachside and village in Vietnam, food vendors tempt with irresistible snacks, piping hot from a wok or refreshingly cool in wraps of lettuce, herbs and jelly-soft rice papers. Most are served with a tangy dipping sauce.

Standout specialties are *cha gio* (tiny crunchy rolls filled with crab meat and chicken), *chao tom* (tender mashed prawn meat grilled on sticks of sweet sugar cane), *nem nuong* (grilled, fried or steamed meatballs), and *goi cuon* (prawns and herbs wrapped in soft, snow-white rice papers). These appetisers will sparkle on your table as a first course or complete Vietnamese spread.

❮ Soft Rice Paper Prawn Rolls (page 14)

Soft Rice Paper Prawn Rolls

Goi cuon

Makes 18

40 g (1½ oz) fine rice
  vermicelli

18 medium-sized green (raw)
  prawns

18 dried rice papers

18 small sprigs of mint or
  coriander

2–3 lettuce leaves, torn into
  18 narrow strips

36 snow-pea sprouts, or garlic
  chives

Vietnamese dipping sauce
  (page 235), to serve

Soak rice vermicelli in water for about 15 minutes to soften. Drain. Shell and devein the prawns and insert a skewer lengthways to keep them straight as they cook.

Bring a large frying pan of lightly salted water to the boil, add the prawns, reduce the heat and simmer for 1 minute. Remove, cover with cold water to prevent overcooking, and drain. Remove the skewers.

Soften rice papers in lukewarm water and spread them on a clean dry cloth. Place a prawn in the centre, topped with a sprig of herbs, lettuce and some of the well-drained rice vermicelli. Fold the sides in over the filling and begin to roll from one side. Tuck two snow-pea sprouts or garlic chives into the roll so their ends protrude by about 4 cm (1½ in). Continue to roll up and gently squeeze. Serve with Vietnamese dipping sauce in a small bowl.

Fresh Rice Paper Rolls

Makes 18

40 g (1½ oz) thin rice
vermicelli or bean threads,
soaked in hot water to soften

2 pieces dried black fungus,
soaked in hot water for
25 minutes

100 g (3½ oz) firm tofu

10-cm (4-in) piece large carrot

10-cm (4-in) piece fresh daikon

½ punnet snow-pea sprouts

2 spring onions

18 × 10-cm (4-in) strips
of lettuce

1 small bunch coriander,
leaves picked

1 small bunch mint, leaves
picked

18 medium-sized dried rice
papers

chilli and lime dipping sauce
(page 237) or light soy
spiced with chopped chilli

To make the filling, drain the vermicelli or bean threads well and cut into 10-cm (4-in) lengths. Next drain the fungus, trim away any woody parts and shred finely. Cut the tofu and vegetables and herbs into slices, then strips.

Working with two or three at a time, soften the rice papers in lukewarm water and place on a clean cloth. Fold the top over and then place the filling onto the rice papers so the ends protrude over the folded edge. Fold the bottom of wrapper over the bundle of filling, and then fold in one side and roll with one end of filling exposed. Arrange them on a platter, with the dipping sauce in a bowl in the middle.

Golden Prawn Cakes

Banh tom

Serves 4–8

100 g (3½ oz) pork fat, diced

500 g (1 lb 2 oz) green (raw) prawn meat

2 spring onions, chopped (keep whites and greens separate)

1 teaspoon grated ginger

1 egg white

2 tablespoons (40 ml/1½ fl oz) fish sauce

½ teaspoon white pepper

oil for frying

6 lettuce leaves, torn into 4-cm (1½-in) strips

sprigs of fresh mint, Vietnamese mint and coriander

Vietnamese or peanut dipping sauce (pages 235 and 238)

Place pork fat, prawn meat, white parts of spring onion, ginger, egg white, fish sauce and pepper in a food processor and grind to a smooth paste. Add 2–3 tablespoons cold water and process until light and smooth.

With wet hands form the mixture into walnut-sized balls and flatten slightly. Heat the oil in a wok or large frying pan over medium–high heat. Fry in two batches for 2 minutes turning once, until golden brown. Drain on paper towel, and transfer to a serving plate.

Assemble before serving, or invite guests to prepare their own. Fold a strip of lettuce around a prawn cake, adding a few herbs and a smear of the sauce. Secure with a toothpick.

Barbecue Sugarcane Prawns

Chao tom

Serves 10–12

2 large cloves garlic, peeled

5 spring onions, white parts only

600 g (1 lb 5 oz) green (raw) prawn meat

2 teaspoons sugar

3 teaspoons fish sauce

2 teaspoons tapioca or potato starch

1 slice bacon, finely diced

1 × 500-g (1-lb 2 oz) can sugarcane sticks, drained

peanut or vegetable oil

Vietnamese dipping sauce (page 235)

In a food processor chop the garlic and onions. Add the prawn meat, sugar, fish sauce and starch and process to a paste. Add the diced bacon and process until very well mixed.

If the sugar cane sticks are large, cut down to pieces about 12-cm (5-in) long. Dry by squeezing in paper towel.

With wet hands, mould portions of the prawn paste around the centre of each stick. Brush lightly with oil and cook slowly on a medium–hot grill, turning often, for about 3½ minutes until cooked with dark-brown flecks on the surface.

Serve at once, with the dipping sauce.

Steamed Prawn Balls

Cha tom

Serves 4–8

500 g (1 lb 2 oz) green (raw) peeled prawns

50 g (1¾ oz) pork fat, finely diced

1 egg, separated

½ teaspoon salt

⅓ teaspoon pepper

1½ tablespoons crisp-fried onions (page 230)

2 teaspoons rice wine (optional)

Place the prawns in a food processor or mortar and grind to a paste. Add the pork fat, egg white, salt, pepper and dried onion and grind again just long enough to mix well. With wet hands form into small walnut-sized balls.

Bring 4 cm (1½ in) water to the boil in a steamer. Cover and reduce to a simmer.

Line the steamer basket with a piece of clean cloth or a round of banana leaf brushed with sesame oil, and spread the balls evenly over it. Mix egg yolk with rice wine and brush over the balls, cover with another piece of cloth or piece of oiled banana leaf (or baking paper), and steam for about 15 minutes.

Serve hot with a dipping sauce or sweet chilli.

Grilled Beef & Peanut Meatballs

Makes 6–8

bamboo skewers, soaked for 20 minutes

peanut or vegetable oil

Vietnamese dipping sauce (page 235)

MEATBALLS

400 g (14 oz) beef mince

2 shallots, finely chopped

2 tablespoons chopped mint or coriander

2 tablespoons finely chopped roasted peanuts

1 clove garlic, finely chopped

1½ tablespoons (30 ml/1 fl oz) coconut cream

3 teaspoons fish sauce

⅓ teaspoon black pepper

1 small red chilli, deseeded and finely chopped

½ teaspoon ground turmeric

Combine all of the meatball ingredients, kneading and squeezing through the fingers until the mixture is well mixed and smooth. With wet hands shape into bite-sized balls and thread three onto each skewer.

Brush lightly with oil and grill on a barbecue, in a hot pan or under the grill, turning often, for about 7 minutes until cooked but a little rare inside.

Serve with Vietnamese dipping sauce or another dipping sauce.

✖ Roasted cashew or macadamia nuts can replace peanuts.

Fried Spring Rolls

Cha gio

Makes 36

200 g (7 oz) canned crab meat,
  picked over for shell

120 g (4 oz) pork mince

2 spring onions (white parts
  only), finely chopped

20 g (¾ oz) bean-thread
  vermicelli, soaked for
  20 minutes in hot water

2 teaspoons fish sauce

salt and white pepper

18 small rice papers

3 tablespoons (60 g/2 oz) sugar

oil for deep-frying

fish sauce or Vietnamese
  dipping sauce (page 235),
  for dipping

Combine crab meat, pork and spring onions in a bowl. Drain the vermicelli well and chop finely. Mix with the crab meat, seasoning with the fish sauce, salt and pepper.

Soften rice papers in lukewarm water sweetened with the sugar and spread on clean kitchen cloths to partially dry. Cut in half. Place a small spoonful of the mixture in the middle of the wrapper and fold the rounded edge over. Fold in two sides and roll up.

In a large frying pan heat the deep oil to low–medium and fry the spring rolls for about 15 minutes, until golden brown and crisp, taking care there is space between the rolls or they will stick together. Drain on paper towel and serve with fish sauce or Vietnamese dipping sauce.

Betel Leaf Parcels

Makes 18

18 fresh or brined betel or grape-vine leaves

400 g (14 oz) pork or beef mince

2 spring onions, finely chopped

2 cloves garlic, finely chopped

3-cm (1¼-in) piece lemongrass, very finely chopped

3 tablespoons (60 ml/2 fl oz) peanut or vegetable oil

2–3 teaspoons fish sauce

salt

large pinch of sugar

1½ tablespoons finely chopped roasted peanuts

Cover brined leaves with boiling water and drain. Trim out the hard central rib and set leaves aside.

In a bowl combine the meat, onions, garlic and lemongrass and mix well. Heat 1½ tablespoons (30 ml/1 fl oz) oil in a wok over high heat and stir-fry the mixture until well browned.

Season to taste with fish sauce, salt and sugar, and fold in the peanuts. Roll a portion of the mixture in each leaf, folding in the ends and sides. Secure with toothpicks or thread several together on bamboo skewers. Brush with oil and brown on a hot grill until the leaf is browned and slightly crisp. Serve with chilli and lime, Vietnamese or peanut dipping sauce.

Vegetarian Golden Spring Rolls

Cha gio chay

Makes 12–24

30 g (1 oz) bean-thread vermicelli, soaked in hot water for 15 minutes

1 punnet fresh Asian mushrooms (shiitake, oyster, black fungus, enoki)

2½ tablespoons (50 ml/1¾ fl oz) peanut or vegetable oil

1 stick celery, finely diced

1 carrot, finely diced

2 spring onions, finely chopped

1½ cups finely chopped cabbage

1½ teaspoons grated fresh ginger

1 teaspoon crushed garlic

1 cup chopped bean sprouts

1½ tablespoons light soy sauce

12 large or 24 small spring-roll wrappers

oil for deep-frying

sesame oil (optional)

Drain the vermicelli and chop finely. Finely chop the mushrooms. Heat the oil in a wok and stir-fry the celery, carrot and spring onions for 1 minute. Add the cabbage, garlic and ginger, and stir-fry for 1 minute. Add the mushrooms, bean sprouts and vermicelli and continue to stir-fry over high heat until the vegetables are cooked. Season to taste with soy sauce, salt and pepper and spread on a plate to cool.

Place a spring-roll wrapper diagonally on a board, add a portion of filling in one corner and fold over. Fold in the sides and shape filling into a roll. Roll up firmly. Moisten the tip with cold water to stick down. **>**

Heat oil for deep-frying over high heat and add 2–3 tablespoons sesame oil (if using). Deep-fry the rolls in batches until golden brown. Drain on paper towel and serve hot.

✳ Wrap salad ingredients and a spring roll in a piece of lettuce.

Spicy Stuffed Crackers

Makes about 20

20 dried tapioca or prawn crackers (or vege crisps)

peanut or vegetable oil for deep-frying

2 cloves garlic, sliced

5 shallots, thinly sliced

100 g (3½ oz) lean pork, chicken or prawn mince

½ cup chopped roasted peanuts

2 tablespoons chopped coriander or Vietnamese mint

3 teaspoons fish sauce

¾ teaspoon sugar

freshly ground black pepper

Heat oil for deep-frying in a wok or large pan and fry the crackers over high heat until they puff up and turn crisp, about 40 seconds. Spread on paper towel to drain.

Pour off the oil and return ½ cup (125 ml/4 fl oz) oil to wok. Fry the garlic and shallots until crisp and golden brown. Drain on paper towel.

Drain the oil from the wok, wipe and return 1 tablespoon (20 ml/¾ fl oz) oil. Fry the mince over a high heat, stirring constantly, until it is browned and almost crisp.

Add peanuts and herbs and season with fish sauce, sugar and black pepper, and lastly stir in the crisp garlic and shallots.

Place a spoonful of the filling on each cracker and serve at once.

Golden Prawn Toast

Banh mi chien tom

Makes about 20

400 g (14 oz) green (raw) prawn meat, diced

60 g (2 oz) pork or bacon fat, diced

10-cm (4-in) piece spring onion, finely chopped

2 egg whites

2 teaspoons fish sauce

white pepper

2 small baguettes, sliced

oil for deep-frying

Place the prawn meat and pork or bacon fat in a food processor and grind to a smooth paste. Add 1 egg white, the spring onion, fish sauce and pepper with 2 tablespoons (40 ml/1 ½ fl oz) water and process until smooth and light. Spread evenly over each slice of bread, tapering towards the crust.

Beat remaining egg white and brush over the filling and the bread crusts.

Heat oil for deep-frying over medium–high heat and carefully slide in half the shrimp toasts, filling-side down. Fry until golden brown, turn and briefly fry the other side.

Drain on paper towel while the remaining toasts are fried. Serve with sweet and sour sauce or Vietnamese dipping sauce (page 235).

Prawn & Cucumber Coins

Makes about 24

60 g (2 oz) pork fat (or the fat from 2 slices of bacon)

3 spring onions, white parts only, chopped

2 cloves garlic, peeled

1-cm piece fresh ginger, peeled

1 hot red chilli, deseeded and chopped

500 g (1 lb 2 oz) green (raw) prawn meat

3 teaspoons chopped fresh coriander

peanut or sesame oil for brushing

2 small cucumbers

fresh herbs, to garnish

chilli and lime dipping sauce (page 237)

Place the pork fat on a plate, cover with cling wrap and microwave for 1 minute. Turn, cover and microwave for a further minute. Chop finely. (If using bacon fat, chop finely but do not cook.)

Place the garlic, onions, ginger and half the chilli in a food processor and grind to a paste. Add the prawn meat and grind until smooth and sticky. Add the pork or bacon fat and coriander and mix in briefly.

Brush two shallow heatproof dishes with oil and cover with the prawn mixture, shaping the edges square with a spatula. Brush lightly with oil and set in a two-tiered steamer over simmering water. Cover and steam for about 8 minutes, until firm. (If you do not have a two-tiered steamer, cook in two batches.)

Remove from the steamer and let stand for a few minutes to cool and firm up. Cut the unpeeled cucumber into slices about 6 mm (¼ in) thick and pat dry with paper towel.

Select a round cookie cutter the same dimension as the cucumber and cut out rounds of the prawn mixture. Set one prawn cake on each piece of cucumber and garnish with a coriander or basil leaf or a small sprig of dill.

Grilled Quail in Betel Leaves

Serves 6

**12 fresh or brined betel
  (or grape-vine) leaves**

6 quails

3 teaspoons dark soy sauce

1 clove garlic, crushed

1 teaspoon sugar

sesame oil for brushing

lime wedges, to serve

Cover betel leaves with boiling water and drain. Trim out the hard central ribs and set leaves aside.

Cut the quails in half and carefully remove the breast meat. Marinate breast pieces in soy, garlic and sugar for 20 minutes.

Wrap a betel leaf around each breast and secure with a toothpick.

Brush lightly with oil and cook quickly over a hot grill, until tender and the leaf is crisp, 1–1½ minutes on each side.

Serve at once, with lime wedges.

Taro & Prawn Patties

Banh tom

Makes about 18

1½ cups grated taro or white sweet potato

½ cup (75 g/2½ oz) rice flour

¼ cup (35 g/1¼ oz) self-raising flour

1 teaspoon baking powder

1 teaspoon salt

½ teaspoon freshly ground black pepper

2 tablespoons chopped coriander

¾ teaspoon crushed ginger

120 g (4 oz) small peeled prawns

oil for shallow-frying

18 lettuce leaves, to serve

fresh mint or coriander, to serve

Peel the taro or sweet potato and grate coarsely or cut into fine matchsticks.

Make a smooth batter by mixing the flours, baking powder, salt and pepper with enough cold water to achieve a creamy consistency. Stir in grated ginger and coriander, the prawns and taro or sweet potato.

Heat about 4 cm (1½ in) oil in a large pan and fry spoonfuls of the mixture over medium–high heat until golden brown and crunchy, turning once or twice. Remove and drain well.

Serve with lettuce leaves and fresh herbs (mint and coriander) for wrapping, along with Vietnamese or peanut dipping sauce (pages 235 and 238).

Chicken & Sausage Skewers

Kim tien ke

Serves 6–8

¾ teaspoon five-spice powder

⅓ teaspoon black pepper

2 tablespoons (40 ml/1½ fl oz) oyster sauce

1 tablespoon (20 ml/¾ fl oz) dark soy sauce or kecap manis

¾ teaspoon fine white sugar

2 tablespoons (40 ml/1½ fl oz) peanut or vegetable oil

400 g (14 oz) chicken breast, cut into 2-cm (¾-in) cubes

3–4 Chinese *lap xuong* sausages

1 bunch spring onions

6–8 bamboo skewers, soaked for 20 minutes

Combine the five-spice, pepper, oyster sauce, soy, sugar and 1 tablespoon (20 ml/¾ fl oz) oil in a large bowl and mix well. Add the chicken and stir until each piece is coated. Cover and refrigerate for 2 hours.

Cut the sausages and white parts of spring onion into 2-cm (¾-in) pieces. Thread the chicken, sausage and spring onion onto skewers, making them large or small, as preferred. Brush with the remaining oil and cook on a medium–hot barbecue plate, under a hot grill or in a non-stick pan, turning frequently, until the chicken is cooked and tender, about 7 minutes.

Chilli Squid

Serves 4–6

2 large cloves garlic

1 large hot red chilli, deseeded and roughly chopped

salt and freshly ground black pepper

2 cleaned squid tubes, pineapple cut (see page 9)

2½ tablespoons (50 ml/1¾ fl oz) peanut oil (or a mix of vegetable and sesame oil)

fish sauce, to taste

finely chopped coriander, to garnish

Place garlic and chilli in a stone mortar and pound to a paste. Add salt and pepper and mix well. Transfer to a bowl, add the squid and mix thoroughly, moistening with a little of the oil. Leave for 15 minutes.

Heat a wok with remaining oil. When very hot sear the squid, turning constantly. Cooking time should be less than 1 minute, longer and the squid will begin to toughen. Season with a splash of fish sauce and garnish with the coriander. Serve hot, with toothpicks.

Grilled Mussels

Makes 18

18 mussels on the half shell

225 g (8 oz) chicken breast,
  cut into cubes

2 spring onions, diced

3-cm (1¼-in) piece lemongrass

1 tablespoon (20 ml/¾ fl oz)
  fish sauce

1½ tablespoons (30 ml/1 fl oz)
  peanut or vegetable oil

2 teaspoons chopped fresh
  coriander

Loosen the mussels from their shells by running a knife beneath them.

Place chicken, spring onion, lemongrass and fish sauce in a food processor and grind to a paste. Spread a little of the mix over each mussel and brush with oil.

Arrange on a heatproof tray and brown under a hot grill until the top is golden and cooked, or place filling-side down in a lightly oiled non-stick pan to cook for about 2½ minutes. Sprinkle with coriander and serve with lemon wedges.

Salads

In Vietnam salad is eaten as a side, added to soup and used to wrap bite-sized pieces of grilled and fried food. A platter of lettuce, crisp salad vegetables and herbs, and a snowy mound of softened rice vermicelli are standard.

The availability of unusual fruit and vegetables, combined with crisp, fresh salad greens lead to many interesting salads. *Cu dau* (yam bean or jicama), which is similar in taste to apple and potato, and green (unripe) papaya with its astringent tang are perfect examples.

The huge thick-skinned pomelo, the largest of the citrus fruits, makes a refreshing salad. Whereas white and black wood-fungus, bean-thread noodles provide a crunchy-chewy texture. Any of the salads that follow can be served Vietnamese-style with rice, as a light meal, or as a side to grilled chicken or pork.

‹ Shredded Chicken & Vietnamese Mint Salad (page 42)

Shredded Chicken
& Vietnamese Mint Salad

Ga xe phei

Serves 4–5

3 chicken drumsticks

3 chicken thigh fillets

1 large red onion, thinly sliced

1 tablespoon (20 ml/¾ fl oz) rice vinegar

salt and freshly ground black pepper

2 large pinches sugar

⅓ cup chopped Vietnamese or other mint

3 lettuce leaves, finely shredded

Place chicken drumsticks and thighs in a saucepan with water to cover. Bring to the boil, reduce heat and simmer for about 25 minutes until tender.

In a small bowl, mix the onion with vinegar and a generous pinch each of salt and sugar, separating the layers of onion. Cover and leave for 20 minutes. Drain the chicken (reserve stock for another recipe), and let the meat cool.

Debone and discard skin, and tear chicken into fine strips. Place the chicken strips in a bowl with the mint leaves and another large pinch each of salt and sugar. Season to taste with pepper and massage lightly into the chicken.

Drain and lightly rinse the onions and fold into the salad. Serve over shredded lettuce.

Bean-thread Noodle Salad

Serves 4–6

180 g (6½ oz) bean-thread
noodles

2 cups bean sprouts

2–3 cups finely shredded
cabbage

½ red and ½ green capsicum,
cut into thin strips

1 carrot, cut into thin strips

2 spring onion greens,
shredded

1 small red salad onion, finely
sliced

3 tablespoons (60 ml/2 fl oz)
salad dressing (page 243)

1 large hot red chilli, deseeded
and finely sliced

sprig of fresh herbs
(coriander, dill, mint, basil,
Vietnamese mint)

Soften bean-thread noodles in boiling water, drain and cut into 8-cm (3-in) lengths.

Blanch bean sprouts in boiling water, let sit for 10 seconds, drain and refresh in ice-cold water for 10 minutes, drain well.

Combine the salad vegetables and noodles in a bowl and add the dressing. Toss well. Cover and chill for 20 minutes. Garnish with chilli and herbs.

Green Papaya Salad

Goi du du

Serves 4–6

½ green (unripe) papaya

3 small shallots, finely sliced

¼ cup chopped coriander

¼ cup chopped mint

¼ cup chopped Vietnamese mint

juice of 1 large lime

2 tablespoons (40 ml/1½ fl oz) fish sauce

2 tablespoons (30 g/1 oz) sugar

3 tablespoons crisp-fried onions or garlic (page 230)

2 tablespoons chopped roasted peanuts (optional)

1 hot red chilli, deseeded and sliced (optional)

Finely shred or coarsely grate the papaya, place in a bowl of cold water for 10 minutes and drain. Mix with the shallots and herbs. Add lime juice, fish sauce and sugar to achieve a salty–sweet, tangy taste. Transfer to a serving dish and garnish with the crisp garlic and onion, and peanuts and chilli if using.

Make Green Papaya Salad into a complete meal by serving with cooked prawns and/or sliced sweet and salty pork belly (page 178) or roast pork (page 167).

Yam Bean Salad

Cu dau goi

Serves 4

1 yam bean, peeled and cut into fine shreds

1 medium-sized carrot, coarsely grated

2 cups fresh bean sprouts, blanched and refreshed

2 tablespoons (40 ml/1½ fl oz) white or rice vinegar

large pinch of salt

2 teaspoons sugar

12 large mint leaves, roughly shredded

5 sprigs fresh coriander, roughly chopped

1 hot red chilli, deseeded and shredded

1 tablespoon crisp-fried onions (page 230)

Combine the salad ingredients in a bowl.

Whisk the vinegar and sugar with 1½ tablespoons (1 fl oz) water and salt. Add the mint, coriander and most of the chilli and toss lightly through the salad. Garnish with remaining chilli and the fried onions.

✻ Nashi, unripe pear, or peeled daikon are good replacements for yam bean.

Pomelo Salad

Serves 4

1 pomelo (or 2 ruby grapefruit)

1 small cucumber, sliced

1 small carrot, coarsely grated

100 g (3½ oz) bean sprouts, blanched and refreshed in ice cold water

2 spring onions, finely sliced

1 small red onion, finely sliced

4 slices roast pork, turkey or chicken, shredded

2 hard-boiled eggs, cut into wedges

2 tablespoons chopped roasted peanuts

sprig of coriander or basil

DRESSING

1 tablespoon dried shrimp

2 tablespoons (1½ fl oz) vegetable oil

1 large clove garlic, peeled

1 small hot red chilli, deseeded

1 tablespoon sugar

2½ tablespoons (1¾ fl oz) fish sauce

1½ tablespoons (1 fl oz) lime juice

2–3 teaspoons peanut oil

Cut the pomelo or grapefruit in half, and then carefully work the flesh out from the skins, saving the skins unbroken, if possible. With a small sharp knife trim the tough skin off the pomelo segments, and then working over a bowl to catch the juices, tear them into bite-sized pieces. Add the prepared salad vegetables, the meat and half the peanuts and toss together. **>**

To make the dressing, fry the dried shrimp in vegetable oil until fragrant, about 1 minute, drain and place in a spice grinder with the garlic and chilli. Grind to a coarse paste. Add the sugar, fish sauce and lime juice and peanut oil and mix well. The dressing is quite tangy.

Toss the dressing through the salad. Serve in the pomelo or grapefruit skins, or bowls. Garnish with the remaining peanuts and hard-boiled eggs. Finish with a sprig of coriander or basil.

Chicken & Cabbage Salad

Ga xe phai

Serves 6

400 g (14 oz) chicken breast

2½ cups shredded Chinese cabbage

2½ cups shredded green cabbage

⅓ cup (80 ml/3 fl oz) salad dressing (page 243), plus extra to serve

1 medium-sized carrot, cut into fine matchsticks

1 large red salad onion, finely sliced

3 tablespoons shredded Vietnamese mint (common mint or coriander)

2½ tablespoons crushed roasted peanuts

Place the chicken in a small saucepan and cover with water. Bring barely to the boil, reduce heat and simmer gently for 10 minutes. Remove from the heat and let sit, covered, for a further 10 minutes. Drain, slice and tear slices into strips.

Coat the chicken and cabbage with the dressing. Add carrot, onion, mint or other herbs and some of the peanuts and toss well. Transfer to a serving dish and garnish with remaining peanuts and a little more dressing.

Rice Noodle Salad with Prawns & Sprouts

Serves 4

150 g (5 oz) dried rice vermicelli or rice sticks

24 cooked prawns, shelled

200 g (7 oz) fresh bean sprouts

1½ tablespoons (30 ml/1 fl oz) peanut oil

3 tablespoons (60 ml/2 fl oz) rice vinegar

1 tablespoon sugar

1 tablespoon (20 ml/¾ fl oz) fish sauce

1 small hot red chilli, finely chopped

1 medium-sized red onion, sliced

2 cloves garlic, finely chopped

4 sprigs fresh coriander or dill, roughly chopped

8 mint or basil leaves, roughly shredded

2–3 tablespoons crisp-fried onions (page 230)

Cook noodles according to the packet directions, rinse in cold water and drain. Cut prawns in half lengthways. Blanch bean sprouts in boiling water, drain and refresh in cold water for 10 minutes.

Whisk together the oil, vinegar, sugar, fish sauce and chilli. Add the sliced onions, garlic and prawns, mixing well. Cover and chill for 10–20 minutes.

Combine well-drained noodles and bean sprouts with the prawn and onions and add the herbs. Toss lightly and serve garnished with crisp onions.

Stir-fried Beef Salad

Serves 4

400 g (14 oz) beef rump or sirloin, very thinly sliced

1 stem lemongrass, very finely chopped

2 tablespoons (40 ml/1½ fl oz) fish sauce

3 cloves garlic, chopped

180 g (6½ oz) rice vermicelli

½ cup chopped roasted peanuts

1 small mignonette or cos lettuce, shredded

1 small cucumber, finely sliced

100 g (3½ oz) bean sprouts, blanched, refreshed and drained

⅓ cup pickled carrot and daikon (page 228)

3 tablespoons (60 ml/2 fl oz) Vietnamese dipping sauce (page 235)

4 sprigs fresh mint, leaves picked

2½ tablespoons (50 ml/1¾ fl oz) peanut or vegetable oil

4 shallots, finely sliced

salt and freshly ground black pepper

Marinate the beef with 1 tablespoon chopped lemongrass and half the fish sauce and garlic for 20 minutes.

Cook the rice vermicelli, drain, rinse and cool. Cut into 8-cm (3-in) lengths and place in a bowl with half the peanuts, the remaining lemongrass, lettuce, cucumber, bean sprouts, carrot, dipping sauce and half the mint. Toss lightly and spread on a serving plate or individual plates.

Heat the oil in a wok over high heat and fry the shallots until well browned. Remove to a plate. Add the beef and stir-fry over very high heat for 1 minute. Add remaining garlic, fish sauce and peanuts and season to taste with salt and pepper. Return onions and mix.

Spread hot beef, onions and frying oil over the salad and serve at once garnished with the remaining mint leaves.

Noodles & Soup Noodles

Bowls of rice noodles are eaten throughout the day from breakfast to late at night. In the north, the day kicks off with a big bowl of Hanoi Soup Noodles or *pho* (pronounced like 'fur') – fragrant with spices and full of beef, rice sticks, herbs and crunchy bean sprouts. Its southern counterpart, Saigon Soup or *hu tieu* (also known as Cambodian Soup) is a mix of meat, chicken or seafood in chicken broth, with rice sticks or flat egg noodles, and fresh salad ingredients on the side.

It seems every region has its own specialty, from cold dishes to rich spicy broths. Not every soup has noodles and not every noodle bowl includes soup. Rice vermicelli, bean threads, fine Chinese-style egg noodles, fresh rice ribbons and soft, snow-white noodle sheets are stir-fried, soft fried and crisp-fried.

‹ Hanoi Soup Noodles (page 58)

Hanoi Soup Noodles

Pho

Serves 4

1 large onion, finely sliced

2 tablespoons (40 ml/1½ fl oz) hot chilli sauce

1.5 L (3 pt 3 fl oz) rich beef stock (page 246)

3 tablespoons (60 ml/2 fl oz) fish sauce

salt and freshly ground black pepper

450 g (1 lb) dried rice-stick noodles, soaked in hot water

400 g (14 oz) rump or sirloin steak, very thinly sliced

½ cup sliced spring onion greens

3 tablespoons chopped coriander

TOPPING

250 g (9 oz) fresh bean sprouts, blanched and drained

1 large hot red chilli, finely sliced (optional)

1 small cucumber, very thinly sliced

1 small bunch mint

1 small bunch basil

2 limes, cut in half

Mix the onion with hot chilli sauce and set aside. Arrange the topping ingredients on a platter and transfer the chilli onions to a small serving dish to take to the table.

Heat the stock to boiling and season with fish sauce, salt and pepper.

Drain rice sticks. Cover with boiling water and let sit for 1 minute. Drain well. Divide noodles between four large soup bowls and top with raw sliced steak, spring onion greens and coriander. Pour the hot stock into each bowl and serve at once. (The stock cooks the meat to deliciously rare.)

At the table, add the toppings as desired and garnish with mint and basil leaves picked from the stems, and a squeeze of lime juice to taste.

✳ If preferred, stir-fry sliced beef before adding to the soup.

Saigon Soup Noodles

Hu tieu

Serves 4

7 cups chicken stock (page 245)

3 chicken thigh fillets, diced

3–4 slices fresh ginger

salt

500 g (1 lb 2 oz) thin egg or rice noodles

3 butterfly pork steaks or 12 green (raw) butterfly prawns (see page 9)

freshly ground black pepper

½ teaspoon five-spice powder

sesame or peanut oil

3 garlic cloves, crushed

2 tablespoons (40 ml/1½ fl oz) fish sauce

¼ cup hot preserved mustard greens, finely sliced

1 cup sliced spring onions

1 tablespoon (20 ml/¾ fl oz) dark soy sauce

250 g (9 oz) fresh bean sprouts, blanched and drained

½ cup fresh coriander sprigs

⅓ cup crisp-fried onions (page 230)

Pour stock into a saucepan and add the chicken and ginger and a pinch of salt. Bring to the boil, reduce heat and simmer for about 25 minutes. Remove chicken, cut into bite-sized pieces, and set aside.

Soak rice noodles in hot water for 10 minutes, or boil egg noodles in lightly salted water for about 6 minutes, until tender. **>**

Season the pork or prawns with salt, pepper and spice powder. Brush with sesame or peanut oil and some of the crushed garlic. Heat a wok and cook the pork for about 2½ minutes on each side, Remove and slice thinly. If using prawns stir-fry for 1½ minutes.

Strain the soup and season with fish sauce.

Reheat the wok with a little more oil and stir-fry the preserved greens and spring onions with remaining garlic over medium–high heat for about 30 seconds. Add chicken and soy sauce and stir-fry briefly. Pile onto a large plate with the sliced pork or prawns, bean sprouts and coriander. Add the drained noodles and garnish with crisp-fried onions.

Serve the soup in four bowls, with the platters of accompaniments.

※ This soup can be served 'dry' with the noodles and accompaniments eaten from one bowl, the soup sipped from another.

Beef & Lettuce Soup with Fresh Rice Noodles

Thit bo rua diep cua

Serves 4

1.5 L (3 pt 3 fl oz) rich beef stock (page 246) or flavour water with instant beef stock seasoning

350 g (10½ oz) fresh rice-roll noodles

200 g (7 oz) thinly sliced rump steak, cut into 5-cm (2-in) strips

3 cups chopped iceberg or cos lettuce

2 teaspoons sesame oil

2 tablespoons (40 ml/1½ fl oz) fish sauce

salt and freshly ground black pepper

Pour stock into a saucepan and bring to the boil.

Cut noodle rolls into 1-cm (⅜-in) wide pieces, place in a bowl and cover with hot water. Gently untangle, rinse and drain. Divide between 4 bowls.

Add sliced beef, lettuce and oil to the hot stock and simmer 1–2 minutes, stirring. Season to taste with fish sauce, salt and pepper and divide evenly between the bowls.

Tart & Tangy Vegetable Beef Soup Noodles

Serves 4

1½ tablespoons instant sour soup (page 249)

2 tablespoons (40 ml/1½ fl oz) peanut or vegetable oil

300 g (10½ oz) coarse beef mince

1 small white onion, thinly sliced

1½ teaspoons tomato paste

½–1 teaspoon chilli flakes or hot chilli sauce

1 small choko or zucchini, diced

2 cups shredded lettuce or silverbeet leaves

350 g (12 oz) rice-stick noodles, soaked in boiling water

2 tablespoons chopped coriander leaves (optional)

3 tablespoons chopped spring onions

1 large hot red chilli, deseeded and sliced

Measure 1.5 L water (3 pt 3 fl oz) into a large saucepan and add the soup-stock paste, stirring to dissolve. Bring to the boil and reduce to a gentle simmer.

Heat the oil in a wok over high heat and sauté the beef and onion with tomato paste and chilli until cooked, about 4 minutes, stirring frequently. Add 2 cups (500 ml/17 fl oz) hot stock and bring to the boil. Add choko or zucchini and simmer for about 3 minutes. Add lettuce or silverbeet and the meat and simmer for a further 3 minutes on gentle heat. Stir into the stock.

Drain noodles, cover with boiling water and let sit for 1 minute, drain and divide between 4 bowls.

Ladle the soup onto the noodles, and garnish with coriander, spring onions and chilli.

Noodle Soup with Seafood Balls & Roast Pork

Bun tom thit nac

Serves 4–5

1.25 L (2 pt 10 fl oz) chicken
stock (page 245)

salt and freshly ground black
pepper

2 tablespoons (40 ml/1½ fl oz)
fish sauce

12–16 frozen squid or prawn
balls, cut in half

3 spring onions, sliced (keep
whites and greens separate)

6 straw or button mushrooms,
sliced

350 g (12 oz) dried rice-stick
noodles, soaked in hot water

100 g (3½ oz) fresh bean
sprouts or rau muong water
vegetable leaves

180 g (6½ oz) roast pork (page
167), thinly sliced

Bring stock to the boil, adding salt and pepper, half of the fish sauce, all of the seafood balls, white parts of spring onions and the mushrooms. Bring back to the boil, reduce heat and simmer for 4–5 minutes. Season to taste with salt and pepper and remaining fish sauce, if needed.

Drain noodles, cover with boiling water and let sit for 1 minute. Drain well.

Evenly distribute noodles, onion greens, bean sprouts and sliced pork between the bowls and top with the hot soup, seafood balls and mushrooms.

Rau muong is a spinach-like vegetable with long tapering leaves and hollow stems.

Pork Rib & Lotus Root Soup

Serves 6

1 kg (2 lb 3 oz) meaty pork
ribs, in 5-cm (2-in) chunks

4 cloves garlic, peeled

salt

5 shallots, peeled

1½ tablespoons (30 ml/1 fl oz)
fish sauce, plus extra
to taste

¼ cup crisp-fried onions
(page 230)

1 piece cassia bark or
cinnamon stick

1 teaspoon black peppercorns

3 spring onions, finely sliced

1 × 350-g (12-oz) can thinly
sliced lotus root, drained

fresh coriander or Vietnamese
mint

1 large hot red chilli, deseeded
and sliced

Place the pork ribs in a bowl. Grind the garlic with 1 teaspoon salt, the shallots and fish sauce to a paste. Rub into the pork, cover and let marinate for 2 hours.

Transfer to a deep saucepan and add about 2 L (4 pt 4 fl oz) water, add the fried onions, cassia or cinnamon, black peppercorns and the white parts of the spring onions and bring to the boil over a medium–high heat. Reduce heat and simmer, skimming the surface from time to time, for about 2½ hours until the meat is falling off the bone. Use a slotted spoon to transfer ribs to a plate.

Strain the soup into a clean saucepan. Add the lotus root and simmer gently while you strip the cooked pork from the bones and chop it into bite-sized pieces. Return the diced pork to the soup and simmer for 2–3 minutes. Taste and adjust seasoning with salt and/or fish sauce.

Serve in deep bowls, distributing meat and lotus root evenly. Add herbs, chilli and spring onion greens.

Crab & Asparagus Soup

Mang tay nau cua

Serves 4–6

1 L (34 fl oz) chicken stock
(page 245)

4 thick white asparagus
spears, thinly sliced on
an angle

180 g (6½ oz) cooked crab
meat

1½ tablespoons (20 g/¾ oz)

cornflour or tapioca starch

3 egg whites, well beaten

salt and freshly ground black
pepper

chopped fresh coriander or
dill, to serve

Bring stock to the boil and add asparagus. Simmer for 2 minutes. Add the crab meat and gently cook for 1 minute.

Stir cornflour or tapioca starch into ⅓ cup (80 ml/3 fl oz) water or cream and pour into the soup. Simmer, stirring often, until the soup thickens and turns milky and translucent.

Remove from the heat, drizzle in the egg whites in a thin stream so they set in threads, and let sit for 1–2 minutes without stirring.

Season to taste and serve garnished with chopped herbs.

Roast Duck & Egg Noodle Soup

Mi vit tiem

Serves 4–5

3 bundles thin egg noodles

salt

1 bunch English or water spinach

½ Chinese roast duck, including neck

2 star anise

1 cinnamon stick

2–3 teaspoons rich beef stock (see page 246)

5–6 button or straw mushrooms, sliced

2 spring onions, finely sliced

dark soy sauce and sugar, to taste

Boil the noodles in lightly salted water for about 6 minutes.

Cut water spinach into 4-cm (1½-in) lengths, discarding tough stem ends.

Debone the duck and place the neck and bones in a saucepan with about 1.5 L (3 pt 3 fl oz) water. Add spices and bring to the boil. Reduce heat and simmer for about 10 minutes. Strain soup into a clean saucepan. Add the soup seasoning, mushrooms and white parts of spring onion and bring back to the boil. Reduce heat and simmer for 2–3 minutes.

Cut the duck meat into small cubes. Add the duck, spinach and noodles to the soup and simmer for 1–2 minutes. Check seasoning and add soy sauce to taste as well as a small pinch of sugar if needed.

Spicy Crab & Pineapple Soup

Canh chua cua

Serves 4–6

1 L (34 fl oz) fish stock (page
244)

160-g (5½-oz) can Vietnamese
crab with spices

1 cup crushed pineapple and
its juice

2 tablespoons (40 ml/1½ fl oz)
fish sauce

salt and freshly ground black
pepper

chopped spring onion greens

Bring the stock to the boil and add the crab and pineapple. Simmer for
2–3 minutes, add fish sauce and seasoning to taste. Add spring onion
greens and serve.

✂ Canned *gia vi cua nau bun rieu* (minced crab with spices) is sold in
well-stocked Asian stores. It can also be used as a filling for fried
spring rolls (page 22).

Seafood Soup with Bean Sprouts

Serves 4-6

1 medium-sized squid tube (hood), ready to use

1 tablespoon (20 ml/¾ fl oz) oil

2 teaspoons tomato paste

1½ teaspoons finely chopped garlic

1.5 L (3 pt 3 fl oz) fish stock (page 244)

12 medium-sized green (raw) prawns, shelled and deveined

200 g (7 oz) firm white fish, in 2-cm (¾-in) cubes

8 cherry tomatoes, cut in half

150 g (5 oz) fresh bean sprouts

2 tablespoons (40 ml/1½ fl oz) fish sauce

1 spring onion, finely sliced

salt and freshly ground black pepper

6 large mint leaves, shredded, or 6 sprigs of dill

1 lemon, cut into wedges

Score the squid and cut into 2-cm (¾-in) squares.

Heat the oil in a saucepan or wok and fry tomato paste and garlic for about 1 minute, until fragrant. Add fish stock and bring to a gentle simmer. Place seafood and tomatoes in the stock and simmer for 6–8 minutes, stirring occasionally, until seafood is tender. Add bean sprouts, fish sauce and spring onion. Check seasoning adding salt and pepper as needed.

Stir in the herbs and serve in deep bowls with lemon for squeezing.

Stir-fried Fresh Rice Noodles with Beef & Bok Choy

Banh pho xao

Serves 3–4

500 g (1 lb 2 oz) fresh rice noodles

300 g (10½ oz) beef rump, fillet or sirloin

3 teaspoons fish sauce

½ teaspoon sugar

1 bunch baby bok choy or broccoli

1 medium-sized carrot, sliced

3 tablespoons (2 fl oz) peanut or vegetable oil

4 shallots, sliced

2 cloves garlic, sliced

3 tablespoons (60 ml/2 fl oz) oyster sauce

1 tablespoon (20 ml/¾ fl oz) light soy or fish sauce

Rinse the noodles in warm water to untangle and soften.

Cut the beef into thin slices, and then into strips. Place in a dish with the fish sauce and sugar and mix well. Leave to marinate for 15 minutes.

Snap off the larger outer leaves of the bok choy and slice the hearts in half. (Cut broccoli into florets, if using.) Place in boiling water for 1½ minutes, remove using a slotted spoon. Add the carrot to the same water for 2 minutes and drain.

Heat 2 tablespoons of the oil in a wok and stir-fry the shallots and garlic over high heat for 1 minute. Push to the side of the pan and add the beef. Stir-fry for about 1 minute, until very lightly cooked. Remove to a plate.

Add the remaining oil followed by the vegetables and cook for 1 minute, stirring.

Pour in the sauces, add the noodles and return the beef. Stir over high heat until noodles and meat are well coated with the sauce and heated through.

Steamed Rice-noodle Rolls with Sausage & Mushroom

Banh cuon

Serves 4

8 dried black mushrooms

450 g (1 lb) fresh rice-noodle roll

2 Chinese sausages

4 spring onions, finely chopped

1½ tablespoons (30 ml/1 fl oz) light soy sauce

2 teaspoons sesame oil

1 tablespoon (20 ml/¾ fl oz) peanut or vegetable oil

Soak the mushrooms in boiling water for 25 minutes.

Place the rice rolls in a steamer over simmering water and steam for 2–3 minutes to soften. Carefully unfold the sheets and spread on a clean tea towel, or lightly oiled cling wrap. Cut each sheet in half.

Very finely slice the sausages, mushrooms and spring onions. Spread evenly over the rolls, leaving 4 cm (1½ in) uncovered at the top. Roll up and arrange side by side on a plate, which fits into the steamer. Pour the soy and oils over the rolls, and steam for 7–8 minutes.

Carefully lift the plate from the steamer and serve at once.

Fried Fish with Fresh Herbs & Soft Noodles

Serves 5–6

300 g (10½ oz) rice vermicelli

650 g (1 lb 7 oz) firm white fish, cut into 3-cm (1¼-in) cubes

2 tablespoons (40 ml/1½ fl oz) fish sauce

¼ cup (35 g/1¼ oz) tapioca or potato starch, cornflour

1 cup (250 ml/8½ fl oz) peanut or vegetable oil

½ cup raw peanuts

2–3 garlic cloves, thinly sliced

3 thin slices fresh ginger, finely shredded

⅓ teaspoon ground turmeric

1 cup fresh herbs (coriander, mint, dill, basil)

crisp-fried onions or garlic (page 230)

1 spring onion, finely shredded

Vietnamese dipping sauce (page 235)

Soak the vermicelli in salted hot water for 10 minutes.

Season the fish with fish sauce and coat lightly with starch or cornflour.

Heat oil in a wok or frying pan over medium–high heat and fry peanuts until golden. Remove with a slotted spoon and drain on paper towel.

In the same oil, fry the garlic until golden brown and remove. Add the ginger and turmeric to the oil with half the fish and fry until golden and cooked through, about 2½ minutes. Using a slotted spoon remove to paper towel. Cook the remaining fish and drain well. **>**

Drain the noodles and spread on a serving platter. Top with the fried fish and garnish with herbs, crisp-fried onions or garlic, spring onion, and the peanuts roughly chopped.

Add a generous splash of Vietnamese dipping sauce over the dish just before serving.

Stir-fried Bean Threads with Crab & Prawns

Mien xao cua tom

Serves 2–4

125 g (4½ oz) bean-thread vermicelli

½ bunch Chinese flowering chives

2 tablespoons (40 ml/1½ fl oz) peanut or vegetable oil

18 medium-sized green (raw) prawns, shelled

200 g (7 oz) cooked crab meat

1 small hot red chilli, deseeded and finely sliced (optional)

½ cup (125 ml/4 fl oz) chicken stock (page 245)

1 teaspoon cornflour or tapioca starch

1½ tablespoons (30 ml/1 fl oz) fish sauce

salt and freshly ground black pepper

fresh coriander, basil or dill, to garnish

Soak the noodles in boiling water to soften. Cut the chives into 4-cm (1½-in) lengths, discarding the tough root ends.

Heat the oil in a wok over high heat and stir-fry the prawns and chives for 1 minute. Add the crab meat and chilli and cook briefly.

Stir cornflour or tapioca starch into the cold stock and pour into the pan, stirring until the sauce thickens and becomes translucent. Add drained bean threads, fish sauce, salt and pepper to taste, and simmer for about 1 minute, stirring occasionally until heated through. Serve with fresh coriander, basil or dill.

Cold Rice Vermicelli with Sweet Pork

Bun bi

Serves 3–4

300 g (10½ oz) sweet and salty pork belly (page 178) or roast pork (page 167)

150 g (5 oz) bean sprouts, blanched and refreshed

2 cloves garlic, chopped

3 thin slices fresh ginger

1 hot red chilli, deseeded and chopped

2½ tablespoons (40 ml/1½ fl oz) fish sauce

juice of 2 small limes or 1 large lemon

1 tablespoon (15 g/½ oz) sugar

1 tablespoon finely chopped mint or coriander

250 g (9 oz) fine rice vermicelli, cooked, drained and cooled

¼ bunch garlic chives, in 4-cm (1½-in) lengths

2–3 tablespoons chopped roasted peanuts

Cut the pork into matchstick strips or thin slices. Drain the bean sprouts.

In a mortar or spice grinder crush the garlic, ginger and chilli to a paste and add the fish sauce, lime or lemon juice, sugar and chopped herbs. Mix well. Check for taste adjusting with extra sugar, fish sauce or citrus as required.

Combine vermicelli with half the sauce. Serve onto plates, with pork, bean sprouts and garlic chives arranged over it. Drizzle on remaining sauce and garnish with the peanuts.

✖ Grilled roast chicken or beef could replace the pork.

Rice, Crêpes
& Rice Rolls

Rice is central to the cuisine of Vietnam. A scoop of tender, steamed long-grain rice or a bowl of sticky rice comes with most hot meals. Turmeric pancakes and thin golden crêpes are made from a batter of coconut milk and rice flour and stuffed with seafood. Rice and rice flour also thicken soups, and are used in sweet and creamy puddings, cakes and snacks.

At rickety outdoor restaurants or around the family table, rice soup, similar to Chinese congee, is a popular simple meal. Over a mound of steamed rice comes an assortment of tasty, chargrilled pork chops, sweet and smoky slices of *xa xiu* roast pork, a couple of grilled chicken wings, or a fried egg, a spoonful of fried onions, slivers of crisp salad vegetables and a generous dollop of spicy sauce.

‹ Clay Pot Chicken & Rice (page 88)

Clay Pot Chicken & Rice

Serves 6

6 chicken thigh fillets, cut into
  2-cm (¾-in) cubes

3 teaspoons fish sauce

3 teaspoons soy sauce

3 teaspoons oyster sauce

1 teaspoon sugar

2 teaspoons sesame oil

4 cloves garlic, chopped

2 cups long-grain rice

3 spring onions, sliced (whites
  and greens separate)

3 cups (750 ml/25 fl oz)
  chicken stock (page 245)

3 tablespoons (60 ml/2 fl oz)
  peanut or vegetable oil

3 shallots, thinly sliced

1½ cups small button
  mushrooms, cut in half

salt

oyster sauce and chopped
  coriander, to serve

Marinate the chicken with the sauces, sugar, sesame oil and half the garlic for 1 hour, stirring occasionally.

Place the rice, remaining garlic, white parts of spring onion, the stock and half the peanut or vegetable oil in a clay pot suitable for stove-top cooking and bring to the boil. Reduce heat, cover with a tight-fitting lid and cook for about 7 minutes.

Heat a wok with the remaining oil and stir-fry the chicken with shallots over high heat until almost cooked, about 6 minutes. Add mushrooms and stir-fry for 30 seconds. Season lightly with salt.

Spread the chicken mixture over the rice, return the lid and continue to cook until rice is tender, about 5 more minutes. Stir, adding half the spring onion greens, cover and allow to rest for 5–6 minutes before serving in the clay pot. Garnish with chopped coriander and swirls of oyster sauce.

Grilled Pork Chop & Onion Rice

Serves 2

2 small pork chops (or thin pork schnitzels)

salt and freshly ground black pepper

1 tablespoon (20 ml/¾ fl oz) spring onion oil (page 231)

1 large onion, finely sliced

peanut or vegetable oil

2–3 cups cooked white rice

3 tablespoons (60 ml/2 fl oz) peanut dipping sauce (page 238)

1 tomato, sliced

½ small cucumber, sliced

1 small carrot, coarsely grated

fresh mint or coriander leaves, to serve

Place pork chops on a cutting board, cover with cling wrap and pound with a meat mallet or rolling pin to spread the meat thin and to tenderise. Leave attached to the chop bone. Season with salt and pepper, brush with spring onion oil and set aside.

Heat a hotplate or heavy non-stick pan over medium–high heat and moisten with peanut or vegetable oil. Sauté the onions until well browned and set aside, keeping warm.

In the same pan cook the pork for about 3½ minutes on each side, basting occasionally with extra spring onion oil, until done.

Divide rice between two plates and top with the pork, fried onions and a spoonful of the peanut sauce. Garnish with tomato, cucumber, carrot and herbs, and serve remaining sauce in small dishes, for dipping.

Roast Pork & Fried Egg Rice Plate

Serves 2

2 eggs

2 cups cooked sticky rice (page 101)

vegetable or sesame oil for frying

180-g (6½-oz) piece *xa xiu* roast pork (page 167), sliced

3 tablespoons (60 ml/2 fl oz) Vietnamese dipping sauce (page 235)

1 cup fresh or marinated bean sprouts (page 229)

2 lettuce leaves, shredded

fresh mint or coriander leaves

Heat a little oil in a small non-stick pan over medium–high heat. Fry the eggs sunny side up, until whites are done and yolks half set.

On two plates spread the rice and cover with pork slices and some of the sauce. Place an egg on top of each, and arrange bean sprouts, lettuce and herbs on the side.

Serve remaining sauce in a small dish.

Omelette Rice Rolls

Trung trang com

Serves 2

2 tablespoons chopped spring onion

oil for frying

1¾ cups cooked sticky rice (page 101)

1 teaspoon fish sauce

salt and freshly ground black pepper

4 eggs

1 tablespoon chopped fresh coriander or Vietnamese mint

peanut dipping sauce (page 238), to serve

In a wok or frying pan sauté the spring onion in 2–3 teaspoons oil over medium–high heat. Add the cooked rice and stir until warmed through, seasoning to taste with fish sauce, salt and pepper.

In a bowl beat eggs with coriander, fish sauce, and a generous pinch of salt and pepper. Heat 2 teaspoons oil in a non-stick pan or omelette pan over medium heat and when the pan is hot pour in half the egg. Cook until firm underneath and barely set on top, occasionally lifting an edge to allow uncooked egg to run onto the hot pan.

Spread half the rice over the omelette and roll up. Increase the heat and brown the omelette on one side, turn, and brown the other. Remove to a plate and cook a second omelette in the same way.

Festive Rice

Serves 6–8

2½ cups long-grain white rice

1 cup (250 ml/8½ fl oz) coconut milk

2 cups (500 ml/17 fl oz) chicken stock (page 245)

6 dried black mushrooms, soaked in boiling water for 25 minutes

2 Chinese sausages

2 tablespoons (40 ml/1½ fl oz) oil

2 spring onions, chopped

1½ tablespoons (30 ml/1 fl oz)

fish sauce

salt and freshly ground black pepper

150 g (5 oz) small shelled cooked prawns

150 g (5 oz) *xa xiu* roast pork (page 167), thinly sliced

3 tablespoons chopped fresh herbs (Vietnamese mint and coriander)

2 eggs, beaten

2 tablespoons crushed roasted peanuts

Combine rice, coconut milk, chicken stock, mushrooms and ½ cup (125 ml/ 4 fl oz) of the soaking water, strained, in a saucepan and bring to the boil. Cover and reduce heat to very low and cook without lifting the lid, for 12 minutes. Remove from the heat and let stand again without uncovering.

Steam or grill the sausages until softened, and slice very thin. Retrieve the mushrooms from the cooked rice and slice them very thin.

Heat the oil in a wok and stir-fry the spring onions over high heat for about 30 seconds. Add the prawns and stir-fry briefly, and then add the rice and half the herbs, and season to taste with fish sauce, salt and pepper.

Meanwhile, to make the crêpes beat 2 eggs in a bowl adding a little water if needed. Heat an omelette pan with a teaspoon of vegetable oil and pour in crêpe batter and allow to spread evenly. Reduce heat to medium–low and cook for about 1 minute. Break into pieces using a spatula.

Spread the rice in a shallow dish and arrange the sliced pork, sausage and broken egg crêpe over the rice. Garnish with remaining herbs and peanuts.

Spicy Rice

Com huong giang

Serves 4

3 cups cooked rice

1½ tablespoons dried shrimp, soaked in hot water for 25 minutes

1½ tablespoons coarsely chopped lemongrass

3 spring onions, sliced (keep whites and greens separate)

2 cloves garlic, peeled

1 hot red chilli, deseeded and roughly chopped

1 hot green chilli, deseeded and roughly chopped

2½ tablespoons (1¾ fl oz) peanut or vegetable oil

100 g (3½ oz) roast pork (page 167), cooked chicken or Chinese sausage, finely diced

2 tablespoons (40 ml/1½ fl oz) fish sauce

salt and freshly ground black pepper

Rub cooked rice with your hands to break up lumps and set aside.

Place shrimp, lemongrass, whites of spring onion, garlic and chilli in a food processor or spice grinder and grind to a coarse paste.

Heat the peanut or vegetable oil in a wok or large pan over high heat and fry the paste for 1 minute, stirring. Add the rice and stir over medium heat until evenly mixed and warmed through, adding a few tablespoons water to moisten the rice if necessary. Stir in the diced meat and season to taste with fish sauce, salt and pepper. Stir-fry for 1 minute until warmed through. Transfer to a serving bowl and garnish with spring onion greens.

Crab Meat & Egg Rice

Serves 4–5

1¾ cups long-grain white rice

1 cup fresh bean sprouts

2 spring onions, chopped (keep whites and greens separate)

1½ tablespoons (30 ml/1 fl oz) vegetable oil

4 egg whites, well beaten

120 g (4 oz) fresh, canned or frozen crab meat, picked over for shell fragments

1 tablespoon (20 ml/¾ fl oz) fish sauce

1 lettuce leaf, finely shredded

salt and white pepper

Measure rice and 2¾ cups water (700 ml/1½ pt) into a saucepan and cover tightly. Bring to the boil, reduce heat to very low and simmer without lifting the lid, for 12 minutes.

Snap roots and seed heads from bean sprouts, and blanch the white part of the sprouts in boiling water. Set aside to drain.

Heat the vegetable oil in a wok and stir-fry onion whites over high heat for 30 seconds. Add the beaten egg whites and crab meat and a teaspoon of fish sauce and cook gently, stirring to break it up into small clumps. Add the cooked rice and mix thoroughly, and then fold in the lettuce, bean sprouts, half of the onion greens, the remaining fish sauce and salt and pepper to taste. Serve garnished with remaining spring onion greens.

Sticky Rice

Xio nep

Serves 4–6

2 cups glutinous rice
3 tablespoons chopped roasted
  peanuts (optional)

Soak the rice for 8 hours, or overnight.

Line a steamer basket with fine cloth and spread the damp rice over it. Steam the rice over gently simmering water for about 40 minutes, sprinkling with a little cold water three times.

Fluff with a fork, transfer to a serving dish, and sprinkle with the peanuts.

Rice Soup with Fish & Chinese Greens

Serves 4

2 small bok choy or tat soi, slit in half

5 cups (1.25 L/2 pt 10 fl oz) chicken stock (page 245)

⅔ cup broken or short-grain rice

5 thin slices fresh ginger, cut into fine shreds

400 g (14 oz) firm white fish, in 1-cm (⅜-in) slices

2 tablespoons (40 ml/1½ fl oz) fish sauce

salt and white pepper

2–3 tablespoons spring onion greens, chopped

1½ tablespoons chopped fresh coriander

3 tablespoons crisp-fried onions or garlic (page 230)

1 large mild red chilli, deseeded and sliced

Blanch the vegetables in boiling water and drain. Set aside.

Bring stock to the boil and add rice and ginger. Reduce heat and cook broken rice for 15 minutes, short-grain for 20 minutes, adding extra water or stock if too much boils away.

Sprinkle almost all of the fish sauce over the sliced fish and add to the soup. Add the vegetables and simmer for about 5 minutes, until ingredients are very tender. Season to taste with remaining fish sauce, salt and white pepper and serve into bowls.

Garnish with coriander, spring onion, crisp-fried onions or garlic and chilli.

Seafood Crêpes

Banh xeo

Makes 6

peanut or vegetable oil for frying

2 tablespoons chopped coriander or spring onion greens

CRÊPES

1 cup (250 ml/8½ fl oz) milk

1 cup (150 g/5 oz) plain flour

1 teaspoon baking powder

salt

large pinch of turmeric

large pinch of sugar

FILLING

250 g (9 oz) medium-sized fresh (raw) shelled prawns

1 medium-sized squid tube (hood)

12 oysters or 6 small scallops

2–3 teaspoons fish sauce

freshly ground black pepper

250 g (9 oz) bean sprouts, blanched and drained

8 straw or small white button mushrooms, thinly sliced

3 spring onions, in 4-cm (1½-in) lengths, shredded

Whisk the crêpe ingredients together with 1 cup (250 ml/8½ fl oz) water to make a thin, creamy batter, adding a little extra water or milk if needed. Set aside.

Cut the prawns in half lengthways. Cut the squid into small pieces and cut the scallops in half. Place seafood in a dish and season generously with fish sauce and black pepper. >

Heat 2 tablespoons (40ml/1½ fl oz) peanut or vegetable oil in a wok or frying pan over high heat and stir-fry bean sprouts, spring onions and mushroom just long enough to soften them. Tip onto a large plate.

Add the seafood and a little extra oil if needed. Stir-fry until barely cooked. Add the vegetables, mix well, and divide into six batches.

Stir chopped coriander or onion greens into crêpe batter.

Heat a few teaspoons vegetable oil in an omelette pan. When hot, pour in a ladleful of the crêpe batter and swirl the pan around so it spreads evenly. Reduce the heat to medium–low. Cover the pan and cook the crêpe for 1–2 minutes and then spread one portion of the filling over.

Fold the crêpe in half, covering the filling, increase heat and cook for about 40 seconds, to brown. A little extra oil drizzled into the pan around the crêpe will help it to crisp. Keep warm in a low oven while the remaining crêpes are cooked, and then serve at once.

Beef & Bean-sprout Rice Soup

Serves 4

1.25 L (2 pt 10 fl oz) chicken or rich beef stock (pages 245 and 246)

⅔ cup broken or short-grain white rice

180 g (6½ oz) beef mince

½ teaspoon black pepper

2 tablespoons (40 ml/1½ fl oz) fish sauce

salt and white pepper

250 g (9 oz) fresh bean sprouts, blanched and drained

½ bunch garlic chives, cut into 3-cm (1¼-in) pieces

Bring the stock to the boil and add the rice. Cook broken rice for 8 minutes, short-grain rice for 12 minutes. Add the beef mince and pepper and stir with wooden chopsticks to break up the meat. Simmer for 10 minutes, stirring frequently. Season with fish sauce, salt and white pepper to taste.

Evenly distribute the bean sprouts and garlic chives between four bowls, and fill with the rice soup.

Seafood

The Vietnamese are skilled fisherman, successful aqua farmers, and inventive cooks. And with one of the world's largest rivers, the Mekong, as its major waterway, and a network of tributaries streams, ponds and canals, it's little wonder seafood and fresh water fish and shellfish have such significance.

Seafood is cooked simply, its natural goodness enhanced by herbs, local pepper, and by the intense flavour contribution of the seafood-based seasonings *nuoc mam* (fish sauce) and *mam tom* or *mam ruoc* (soft shrimp paste).

< Whole Fish Steamed with Lemongrass (page 110)

Whole Fish Steamed with Lemongrass

Ca hap xa

Serves 4–6

1.5 kg whole sweet lip or red emperor

salt and freshly ground black pepper

2 teaspoons fish sauce (optional)

2 plump stem lemongrasss

5–6 sprigs fresh coriander or dill

2-cm (¾-in) piece fresh young ginger

1½ tablespoons (30 ml/1 fl oz) light soy or oyster sauce (optional)

Rinse the fish well and pat dry with paper towel. With a sharp knife make several deep slashes across each side. Season lightly with salt, black pepper and half of the fish sauce (if using).

Slit the stem lemongrasss in half and place three pieces in the base of a steamer along with a few stems of coriander or dill and about 5 cm (2 in) warm water. Set on medium heat.

Cut the ginger and remaining lemongrass into fine strips. Set the fish on a plate, brushed with oil, and place into the steamer. Evenly scatter the shredded lemongrass and ginger, placing some in the cavity of the fish. Sprinkle over a little more oil. Steam for 10 minutes, and then add the fish sauce (if using), and the coriander or dill leaves and continue to steam until done, 6–8 minutes. Carefully lift the plate from the steamer and scrape away the ginger and lemongrass. Add oyster sauce (if using) and serve.

Prawns Stir-fried with Lemongrass & Chilli

Tom riem xo voi

Serves 4

2 tablespoons (40 ml/1½ fl oz) peanut or vegetable oil

1 large onion, sliced

24 medium-sized fresh (raw) prawns, shelled and deveined

1 plump stem lemongrass, trimmed and very finely sliced

1 large hot red chilli, deseeded and sliced

1 tablespoon (20 ml/¾ fl oz) fish sauce

2 teaspoons light soy sauce

¾ teaspoon sugar

Heat the oil in a wok and stir-fry the onion over high heat until golden. Remove to a plate.

Reheat the wok, adding a little more oil if needed, and stir-fry the prawns with lemongrass and chilli until the prawns are pink and lemongrass crisp, about 3 minutes. Return the onions, add fish and soy sauces and the sugar and stir well.

Serve over softened rice vermicelli, rice-stick noodles or plain white rice.

Sticky Prawns with Chilli & Sesame Seeds

Serves 2–4

3 teaspoons fish sauce

1 small clove garlic, crushed

12 large green (raw) prawns

2 egg whites

¾ cup (110 g/4 oz) potato starch or cornflour

oil for deep frying

3 tablespoons (60 ml/2 fl oz) caramel sauce (page 236)

1 small red chilli, deseeded and chopped

2 teaspoons sesame seeds

In a small bowl combine fish sauce, garlic and 2–3 teaspoons water and mix well. Add the prawns and stir to coat evenly. Cover and marinate for 20 minutes.

Dry the prawns on paper towel.

Whip the egg whites to soft peaks and stir in ½ cup (85 g/3 oz) potato starch or cornflour and a tablespoon or two of cold water to make a batter. Coat prawns lightly with the remaining potato starch or cornflour.

In a wok or large pan heat the oil to medium–hot for deep frying, and have ready some paper towel for draining the fried prawns. When the oil is hot, hold each prawn by the tail, drag through the oil and carefully slide into the oil to cook for about 2½ minutes, until golden brown and cooked through. (For best results cook prawns in two batches.)

Drain the hot oil into a metal container and set aside.

Return the wok or pan to medium heat. Add the caramel, chilli and sesame seeds and cook until foamy. Add the prawns and gently stir to coat with the glaze.

Prawns with Lime & Pepper

Serves 3–4

12 large green (raw) prawns
 in their shells

2 teaspoons very finely
 chopped lemongrass

grated zest and juice of 1 large
 lime

1 teaspoon crushed garlic

1½ teaspoons fish sauce

½ teaspoon ground black
 pepper

peanut or vegetable oil

Cut unshelled prawns lengthways in half from the underside without cutting right through. Open out and press flat so the two parts of the shell are on one side, and the meat on the other.

In a stone mortar pound the lemongrass until reasonably smooth. Combine with the lime zest, garlic, fish sauce, pepper and 2–3 teaspoons oil and brush over the prawn meat. Cook, meat down on a hot grill plate for about 2½ minutes, turn and briefly cook the shell side.

Serve hot, sprinkled with the lime juice.

Crispy Salt & Pepper Prawns

Serves 4–6

2 tablespoons fine table salt

1 teaspoon black pepper

2 teaspoons five-spice powder

1 teaspoon fine white sugar

1 small dried red chilli,
deseeded and finely crushed

36 small green (raw) prawns
in their shells

⅓ cup (50 g/1¾ oz) tapioca or
potato starch, or cornflour

oil for deep frying

Heat a wok and add the salt. Warm over medium heat for 1 minute. Remove from the heat and add the pepper, five-spice, sugar and chilli. Swirl the mixture around in the wok for a few seconds, and then tip into a dish and set aside to cool.

Coat the prawns lightly with the starch or cornflour.

Heat oil for deep-frying in a wok and fry the prawns in three or four batches until crisp (about 2½ minutes).

Drain the oil and wipe the inside of the wok with paper towel to remove excess oil. Return the prawns, sprinkle on the spice mixture and toss over high heat until well coated. Serve at once, to be eaten, shell and all.

Stir-fried Prawns with Onions

Serves 4

20 medium-sized green
  (raw) prawns, shelled and
  deveined with tail intact

2½ tablespoons (50 ml/1¾ fl oz)
  vegetable or peanut oil

1 bunch spring onions or
  2 medium-sized onions,
  finely sliced

3 cloves garlic, sliced

3 tablespoons (60 ml/2 fl oz)
  caramel sauce (page 236)

4 slices fresh ginger, finely
  chopped

fish sauce or salt, to taste

With a small sharp knife cut deeply along the centre back of each prawn to butterfly.

Heat 1 tablespoon (20 ml/¾ fl oz) oil in a wok and stir-fry the spring onions or onion until cooked and softened, about 2 minutes. Spread on a plate and return the wok to the heat. Add remaining oil to the wok and stir-fry the garlic for 40 seconds. Remove and discard garlic.

Add the prawns to the hot, garlic-flavoured oil and stir-fry over high heat for 2 minutes, until they change colour and begin to curl up. Add the caramel sauce and ginger and continue to stir-fry until the prawns are glazed. Season to taste with fish sauce or salt and add a tablespoon or two of water to make a light sauce. Spread prawns over the onions, and serve at once.

Stir-fried Fish with Bamboo Shoots & Mushroom

Serves 3–4

450 g (1 lb) firm fish, cut into 2-cm (¾-in) cubes

salt and freshly ground black pepper

¾ cup sliced bamboo shoots, drained

2½ tablespoons (50 ml/1¾ fl oz) peanut or vegetable oil

3 shallots or 1 small onion, sliced

8–10 small button or straw mushrooms, cut in half

1 tablespoon fish sauce

chopped fresh coriander or basil, to serve

Season the fish with salt and pepper.

Blanch bamboo shoots in boiling water and tip into a colander to drain.

Heat the peanut or vegetable oil in a wok and stir-fry the fish and onion over high heat for about 2 minutes, until browned and almost cooked. Remove to a plate.

Reheat the wok and stir-fry bamboo shoots and mushrooms over high heat for about 1 minute. Return the fish to the wok and add 2 teaspoons fish sauce. Cook on reduced heat for 2–3 minutes, check seasoning and adding more fish sauce if needed. Serve garnished with chopped herbs.

Grilled Fish with Shrimp Sauce & Rice Papers

Serves 4

4 snapper or John Dory fillets, skin off

1 tablespoon very finely chopped lemongrass

2 teaspoons finely chopped garlic

2 teaspoons grated fresh ginger

1 small hot red chilli, deseeded and chopped

½ teaspoon black pepper

½ teaspoon salt

peanut or vegetable oil

12 dried rice papers

6 small soft lettuce leaves

1 cup pickled carrot and daikon (page 228)

⅓ cup (80ml/3 fl oz) shrimp paste dipping sauce (page 240)

Pat the fish dry with paper towel.

Place lemongrass, garlic, ginger, chilli, pepper and salt in a mortar or spice grinder and grind to a paste adding 2 tablespoons (1½ fl oz) vegetable oil. Brush evenly over the fish, cover and refrigerate for 2 hours.

Heat a grill or barbecue and cook the fish for about 2½ minutes on each side. Break fish into pieces and serve wrapped in rice papers lined with lettuce, and well-drained pickled carrot and daikon. Serve with shrimp paste sauce for dipping.

Simmered Mackerel

Serves 4

4 mackerel cutlets

⅔ cup (160 ml/5½ fl oz)
  caramel sauce (page 236)

2 cloves garlic, finely chopped

fresh coriander or mint,
  for garnish

Place mackerel in a heavy pan and add the caramel sauce, ½ cup (125 ml/ 4 fl oz) water and garlic. Cover and simmer gently for about 20 minutes, basting from time to time, and carefully turning the fish once. Lift fish onto plates and keep warm.

Return pan to heat and reduce liquid to make a sauce. To thicken sauce, add 2 teaspoons corn flour mixed with 2 tablespoons (40 ml/1½ fl oz) cold water.

Serve fish with steamed or fried rice with the sauce poured over. Garnish with the herbs.

Turmeric-flavoured Grilled Fish

Serves 4

4 × 120-g (4 oz) mackerel
fillets, skin on

3-cm (1¼-in) piece galangal,
peeled and roughly chopped

1.5-cm (⅝-in) piece fresh
turmeric or 1 teaspoon
ground turmeric

2 shallots or 1 small onion,
chopped

4 sprigs fresh dill, chopped

1 tablespoon (20 ml/¾ fl oz)
fish sauce

2 teaspoons soft shrimp paste

½ teaspoon black pepper

2½ tablespoons (50 ml/1¾ fl oz)
peanut or vegetable oil

1 large lime or lemon

With a sharp knife slash the skin of the fish.

Combine the galangal, turmeric, onion and dill in a food processor or spice grinder and grind to a paste. Add fish sauce, shrimp paste and pepper and half the oil and grind again until well mixed. Spread evenly over both sides of the fish, cover and refrigerate for 1 hour.

Scrape off the excess marinade, brush fish with remaining oil and grill for about 2 minutes on each side, until cooked. Serve at once, with lime or lemon wedges for squeezing.

Grilled Fish Sticks

Cha ca nuoc leo

Serves 5–6

1 teaspoon soft shrimp paste

2½ tablespoons (50 ml/1¾ fl oz) fish sauce

1 teaspoon sugar

3 teaspoons rice wine

1 teaspoon black pepper

2 teaspoons finely chopped garlic

2 teaspoons finely chopped ginger

¼ teaspoon ground turmeric (optional)

2 tablespoons peanut or vegetable oil, plus extra for brushing

650 g (1 lb 7 oz) thick, firm fish fillets (tuna, mackerel, swordfish), cut into 3-cm (1¼-in) cubes

125 g (4½ oz) pork fat or speck (smoked bacon fat)

3 tablespoons finely chopped roasted peanuts

2 tablespoons chopped fresh coriander

In a bowl combine shrimp paste, fish sauce, sugar, rice wine, pepper, garlic, ginger, turmeric (if using) and oil. Mix well. Add the fish pieces and stir to coat. Cover and refrigerate for 1–2 hours.

Cut pork fat or speck into thin slices and then into 3-cm (1¼-in) squares. Thread the fish pieces onto bamboo skewers, larding between them with the fat or bacon. Brush with oil and cook, turning often, on a barbecue hot plate or under a grill, until crisp and well browned on the surface, about 4 minutes. Sprinkle with the peanuts and coriander and serve.

Fish Simmered with Tamarind & Pineapple

Serves 6

4 thick mackerel, swordfish
  or flathead steaks

salt

1 fish head and frame

1 stem lemongrass, bruised

1½ tablespoons tamarind purée

1½ tablespoons sugar,
  or to taste

1 Asian green melon

1 choko or zucchini

2 thick slices fresh pineapple

2 tomatoes, cut into wedges

1 hot red chilli, deseeded and
  cut in half

2 tablespoons (40ml/1½ fl oz)
  fish sauce

fresh coriander, dill or
  Vietnamese mint

Cut the fish into 3-cm (1¼-in) chunks and season lightly with salt.

Place fish head and frame into a saucepan with 5 cups water (2 pt 10 fl oz) and the lemongrass. Bring to the boil, reduce heat and simmer gently for about 12 minutes. Strain into another saucepan and add the tamarind and sugar. Bring to the boil and reduce heat.

Peel the melon and choko or zucchini and cut into chunks. Add to the stock with the pineapple, tomatoes and chilli and bring back to the boil. Simmer for about 5 minutes. Add the fish and simmer for about 10 minutes, until the fish is tender. Season to taste with extra fish sauce. Serve in deep bowls, garnished with the herbs.

Chargrilled Snapper

Serves 4

4 snapper fillets, skin on

1 teaspoon soft shrimp paste (optional)

3 teaspoons fish sauce

1 tablespoon finely chopped garlic

1 tablespoon very finely chopped lemongrass

1 teaspoon ground turmeric

½ teaspoon black pepper

juice and grated zest of ½ lemon

1 tablespoon (20 ml/¾ fl oz) oil

4 lettuce leaves, finely shredded

1½ cups fresh mixed herbs (dill, coriander, basil, mint)

3 tablespoons (60 ml/2 fl oz) spring onion oil (page 231)

2 tablespoons chopped roasted peanuts or sesame seeds

With a very sharp knife make several cuts across the skin side of the fish.

In a bowl combine shrimp paste (if using), fish sauce, garlic, lemongrass, turmeric, pepper and the lemon juice and zest. Brush over both sides of the fish, cover and let sit for 20 minutes.

Heat a barbecue hotplate or heavy non-stick pan and moisten lightly with oil. Chargrill the fish over high heat for about 2 minutes each side, until cooked. Arrange on the lettuce and finish with the herbs, spring onion oil, and the peanuts or sesame seeds.

Fresh Oysters with Herbs

Serves 2–4

24 large fresh oysters on the half shell

2 teaspoons finely chopped garlic

3 hot red chillies, deseeded and finely chopped

2 teaspoons finely chopped fresh ginger

2 tablespoons finely chopped dill or coriander leaves

juice and grated zest of 1 large lime

salt and freshly ground black pepper

2 tablespoons (40 ml/1½ fl oz) fish sauce

1–2 teaspoons sugar

Arrange the oysters on a plate over rock salt or a napkin.

In a bowl combine the garlic, chilli, ginger, herbs and lime zest and add a pinch each of salt and black pepper. Mix well. Spoon a little of the mixture onto each oyster.

Mix lime juice with fish sauce and sugar to taste, making it slightly tangy. Add a few teaspoons of water. Spoon evenly over the oysters and serve at once.

Chicken, Duck & Quail

Ducks, chickens and quails are sold live in Vietnamese food markets, to be prepared on demand for discerning shoppers who want their poultry no other way than absolutely fresh.

At home and in restaurant kitchens, poultry is grilled over smoky charcoal fires, seared on hot iron plates, tossed in red-hot woks, or slow simmered to succulent tenderness in clay pots with fragrant spices.

Aromatic herbs, crisp lettuce, tangy dipping sauces and pickled vegetables counterbalance the sweetness of chicken and the richness of duck and quail.

‹ Stir-fried Chicken in Lettuce Wraps (page 132)

Stir-fried Chicken in Lettuce Wraps

Serves 4

300 g (10½ oz) chicken breast

2 tablespoons (40 ml/1½ fl oz) sweet chilli sauce

2 teaspoons dark soy sauce

¼ teaspoon freshly ground black pepper

40 g (1½ oz) fine rice vermicelli, softened in hot water

1 medium-sized carrot, grated

1 cucumber, cut into matchstick strips

8 large lettuce leaves, cut into 3–4 pieces

1 small bunch fresh mint or coriander

2 tablespoons (40 ml/1½ fl oz) spring onion oil (page 231)

salt

2 tablespoons (40 ml/1½ fl oz) vegetable or peanut oil

Thinly slice the chicken and cut into strips 1 cm (⅜ in) wide. In a bowl combine the sweet chilli, soy and pepper and mix well. Add the chicken, stir to coat, and marinate for 20 minutes.

Arrange the well-drained rice vermicelli, carrot and cucumber on a platter with the lettuce leaves and herbs. Sprinkle spring onion oil over the rice vermicelli, and season with salt.

Heat the oil in a wok and when very hot add the chicken. Stir-fry over high heat until lightly crisped, about 2 minutes. Serve on a separate plate. Fill pieces of lettuce with some of each ingredient. Roll up and eat.

Chicken with Lemongrass & Chilli

Ga xao xa ot

Serves 4

8 chicken legs, skin on

3 tablespoons (60 ml/2 fl oz) peanut or vegetable oil

2 small onions, sliced

4 cloves garlic, peeled

1 thick stem lemongrass, trimmed and finely sliced

2 medium-sized red chillies, deseeded and cut in half

2 tablespoons (40 ml/1½ fl oz) fish sauce

2 tablespoons (40 ml/1½ fl oz) caramel sauce (page 236)

salt and freshly ground black pepper

Rinse, drain and dry the chicken legs. Make several deep cuts in the thickest part of the meat.

Heat half the peanut or vegetable oil in a wok or saucepan and sauté the onions over high heat until lightly browned. Add the garlic, lemongrass and chilli and sauté briefly. Remove to a plate.

Reheat the wok and add remaining oil. Brown the chicken legs for about 5 minutes, turning often. Return the onion mixture and add the fish and caramel sauces and 1 cup (250 ml/8½ fl oz) water. Bring to the boil, cover and reduce to a simmer. Cook the chicken until tender, about 35 minutes, turning from time to time. Check seasoning adding salt and pepper to taste.

Sweet & Sticky Chicken with Ginger

Thit ga kho gung

Serves 4–6

½ cup (110 g/4 oz) sugar

½ cup (125 ml/4 fl oz) fish sauce

750 g (1 lb 10 oz) chicken thigh fillets

2-cm (¾-in) piece fresh ginger, finely shredded

¾ teaspoon freshly ground black pepper

Melt sugar in a saucepan until golden brown and syrupy. Remove from the heat and carefully add the fish sauce. It will bubble fiercely and the sugar may set into a soft toffee. Add 1 cup (250 ml/8½ fl oz) water and return to the heat, simmering for 2–3 minutes until the toffee has dissolved.

Cut each piece of chicken in half and add to the syrup with ginger and pepper. Simmer gently for about 20 minutes, until the chicken is tender.

Chicken Stuffed with Sticky Rice

Ga rut xuong nhoi nep

Serves 6–8

1 x 1.5-kg (3-lb 5-oz) chicken

1¾ cups glutinous rice

½ cup (125 ml/4 fl oz) coconut cream

2 teaspoons chicken stock powder

4 dried black mushrooms, soaked in hot water for 25 minutes

2 tablespoons small dried shrimp, soaked in hot water for 25 minutes

2 spring onions, chopped

¼ cup chopped bamboo shoot or water chestnuts

¼ cup roasted peanuts, chopped

1 Chinese *lap xuong* sausage, finely sliced

salt and freshly ground black pepper

½ lemon

metal or bamboo skewers, soaked for 30 minutes

3 cups (750 ml/25 fl oz) oil

With a small sharp knife slit along the length of the chicken's backbone and then debone by scraping the meat from the bones, until all that remains are the leg bones and the middle and lower bones in the wings. Carefully scrape the meat halfway down the leg bones and chop off the bones in the middle. Season the boned chicken with salt and set aside.

Strain and reserve the water used to soak mushrooms and shrimp to make 1½ cups (375 ml/12½ fl oz).

In a saucepan combine the rice, coconut cream, reserved mushroom and shrimp liquid, chicken stock powder, the mushrooms, finely diced, and the soaked dried shrimp.

Bring to the boil, cover tightly, reduce heat to very low and simmer, covered, for about 20 minutes. Add the spring onions, bamboo shoots or water chestnuts, peanuts and sausage. Season to taste with salt and pepper.

Bring the cut edges of the chicken together and secure with metal or bamboo skewers. Stuff with the rice mixture, shaping the chicken to its original form by gently easing the filling into the drumstick and breast cavities. Season the chicken with the cut lemon and salt, then pat dry with paper towel.

Heat the oil in a clean, dry wok over medium–high heat. When the oil is hot, add the chicken and cook until browned and cooked through, about 12 minutes, carefully turning several times and basting with the hot oil. Cut into slices to serve.

Crunchy Chicken & Vegetables

Serves 4–6

4 chicken thigh fillets, cut into 2-cm (¾-in) cubes

⅓ teaspoon black pepper

3 teaspoons fish sauce

2 cups (500 ml/17 fl oz) peanut or vegetable oil

1 carrot, sliced

1 stick celery, chopped

12 small florets broccoli or cauliflower

1 small red onion, cut into thin wedges

½ red capsicum, cut into 2-cm (¾-in) squares

3 spring onions, using only 10 cm (4 in) of the greens, sliced

2 small ripe tomatoes, in wedges

¼ cup tapioca (35 g/1¼ oz) or potato starch, or cornflour

½ cup (125 ml/4 fl oz) chicken stock (page 245)

2 tablespoons (40 ml/1½ fl oz) oyster sauce

½ teaspoon sugar

Place chicken in a bowl, add pepper and fish sauce, mix well and leave to marinate for 10 minutes.

Heat a wok with 1 tablespoon (20 ml/¾ fl oz) oil and stir-fry carrot, celery, broccoli, onion and capsicum for 1 minute. >

Add 2 tablespoons (40 ml/1½ fl oz) water, cover and cook for about 2 minutes. Uncover the wok, increase heat to high and add spring onions and tomatoes. Stir-fry for 30–40 seconds, and transfer to a plate.

Rinse and dry the wok. Return to high heat and add remaining peanut or vegetable oil.

Coat the chicken thickly in tapioca or potato starch, or cornflour and fry in the oil a few pieces at a time, until golden brown and cooked through, about 3 minutes. Set chicken aside and drain the wok.

Stir 2 teaspoons starch or cornflour into the stock.

Rinse and dry the wok and return 2 tablespoons (40 ml/1½ fl oz) of the hot oil. Reheat the vegetables and add the chicken stock and starch mixture, stirring until the sauce thickens and becomes translucent. Add oyster sauce and sugar and check seasonings adding a little fish sauce or extra oyster sauce, to taste. Stir in the fried chicken and warm through just long enough to coat with the sauce.

Serve with plain steamed rice.

Barbecued Chicken

Serves 4

1 stem lemongrass, trimmed
and roughly chopped

4 cloves garlic

1½ teaspoons salt

1 teaspoon pepper

juice of ½ lemon

4 chicken marylands
(drumstick and thigh),
skin on

2 tablespoons honey

2 tablespoons (40 ml/1½ fl oz)
boiling water

Grind lemongrass, garlic, salt and pepper in a food processor and add the lemon juice.

Spread over the chicken, cover and marinate for 1 hour.

In a small bowl, combine honey and boiling water, stirring to dissolve.

Heat a charcoal barbecue or grill to high. Put the chicken on to cook, turning after 4 minutes. Brush with the honey mixture and continue to cook, turn and baste until the chicken is browned and cooked through, about 8 minutes.

✳ Prick the chicken with a sharp skewer to allow seasonings to penetrate and fat to run off during cooking.

Grilled Pepper-crusted Chicken Breast

Serves 4

2 large chicken breasts

1 ⅓ teaspoons dry green peppercorns

2 cloves garlic, thinly sliced

1 small hot red chilli, deseeded and chopped

1 spring onion, chopped

½ teaspoon salt

3 tablespoons (60 ml/2 fl oz) oil

1 large lime

Cut each chicken breast into 1-cm (⅜-in) slices, place on cling wrap or baking paper, cover with more cling wrap or baking paper and use a meat mallet or rolling pin to flatten the chicken without tearing it.

Pound peppercorns in a mortar or spice grinder and tip into a bowl. Pound garlic, chilli and onion to a paste with the salt, add the ground pepper and oil and brush over the chicken.

Grill the chicken over glowing charcoal for about 2½ minutes, turning frequently and brushing with any remaining marinade. Serve with lime wedges.

✕ Try using a wire toaster to grill chicken (see pages 5–6).

Crispy Five-spice Chicken

Serves 4–6

1 × 1.6-kg (3 lb 8-oz) whole chicken

1½ (30 ml/1 fl oz) tablespoons rice wine

2 tablespoons (40 ml/1½ fl oz) light soy sauce

1 tablespoon (20 ml/¾ fl oz) dark soy sauce

1 tablespoon (15 g/½ oz) sugar

2 teaspoons grated fresh ginger

2 teaspoons five-spice powder

1½ tablespoons (30 ml/1 fl oz) sesame or peanut oil

4 cups (34 fl oz) oil for deep frying

five-spice salt (page 241) or hoisin sauce

Cut the chicken in half, rinse, drain and pat dry. Prick the legs and thighs with a skewer.

In a bowl combine the wine, soy sauces, sugar, ginger, five-spice powder and sesame or peanut oil. Brush evenly over the chicken on all sides, cover and refrigerate overnight, turning and basting once or twice.

Heat the oven to 240°C (460°F).

Set a rack in an oven tray lined with aluminum foil. Place chicken on the rack to roast for 15 minutes on each side. Remove and let sit for 30 minutes for the skin to dry.

Heat the oil to very hot and carefully add one piece of chicken skin-side down. Cook turning once or twice, until crisp and well browned. Keep warm while the other half is cooked.

Use a cleaver to chop the chicken into bite-sized pieces, cutting through the bone. Serve with five-spice salt or hoisin sauce for dipping.

Tangy Fried Chicken

Ga chien

Serves 3–4

4 chicken thigh fillets, diced

2 tablespoons (40 ml/1½ fl oz) fish sauce

⅓ teaspoon black pepper

1 stem lemongrass, trimmed and finely chopped

2-cm (¾-in) piece fresh ginger, finely shredded

2 tablespoons (40 ml/1½ fl oz) rice vinegar

1 teaspoon sugar

2 tablespoons (40 ml/1½ fl oz) peanut or vegetable oil

1 medium-sized onion, sliced

¼ cup sliced spring onion greens

2 large cloves garlic, sliced

½ cup (125ml/ 4 fl oz) chicken stock (page 245)

2 teaspoons cornflour

salt and freshly ground black pepper

Marinate the chicken with half the fish sauce and all of the pepper and lemongrass for 20 minutes. In another bowl combine ginger, vinegar and sugar.

Heat oil in a wok or saucepan and brown the onions. Remove to a plate using a slotted spoon. Stir-fry until lightly browned. Add the garlic and spring onion greens and stir-fry on medium heat for about 2 minutes. Cover and cook a further 10 minutes, stirring once or twice. Add the ginger and its marinade, and chicken stock mixed with the cornflour and simmer, stirring frequently, until the chicken is tender and glazed with the sauce. Stir in remaining fish sauce and season to taste with salt and pepper.

Chicken & Taro Curry

Cari ga khoai mon

Serves 6

800 g (1 lb 12 oz) chicken
  thigh fillets

2 tablespoons (40 ml/1½ fl oz)
  fish sauce

⅓ cup (80 ml/3 fl oz) peanut
  or vegetable oil

3–4 small pickling onions,
  cut in half

1 stem lemongrass, roughly
  chopped

3 cloves garlic, sliced

1½ tablespoons mild curry
  powder

1 small cinnamon stick

8–10 dried or fresh curry
  leaves (optional)

1 × 400-ml (13½-fl oz) can
  coconut cream

450 g (1 lb) taro, in 1.5-cm
  (⅝-in) cubes

salt

fresh coriander or mint,
  to garnish

Cut each chicken thigh fillet into three pieces. Season with half of the fish sauce and let sit for 10 minutes.

Heat half of the oil in a large saucepan and brown the chicken over high heat, turning several times. Remove to a plate.

Add the remaining oil and brown the onions, turning often, and then add the garlic and lemongrass and fry briefly. Return the chicken, sprinkle on the curry powder and add the cinnamon stick, curry leaves and remaining fish sauce. Stir to coat the chicken with the spices and then add the coconut cream, 1 cup (250 ml/8½ fl oz) water, the cubed taro and a large pinch of salt. Cover and bring to the boil, reduce heat and simmer for about 35 minutes, until chicken is tender and taro cooked through. Check for seasoning and garnish with coriander or mint.

Glazed Chicken Wings with Pickled Bean Sprouts

Canh ga chien dua

Serves 4–6

6 large chicken wings

¼ cup (55 g/2 oz) fine white sugar

3 tablespoons (60 ml/2 fl oz) fish sauce

1 tablespoon finely shredded fresh ginger

2 spring onions, finely sliced

2 cups bean sprouts

3 teaspoons sugar

1 teaspoon salt

2 tablespoons (40 ml/1½ fl oz) rice vinegar

1 small red chilli, deseeded and finely sliced or chopped

1–2 large lettuce leaves, shredded

Separate chicken wings at the joints and set aside.

Melt the sugar in a wok or saucepan and gently cook until golden brown. Remove from the heat and carefully add the fish sauce and 2 tablespoons (40 ml/1½ fl oz) water.

Return to the heat to simmer for 2 minutes, and then add the chicken wings, shredded ginger and the white parts of the spring onion and some of the greens. Cover and simmer gently for 20 minutes, turning the wings from time to time, until the sauce is reduced to a sticky glaze. **>**

In the meantime, blanch the bean sprouts in boiling water and drain well. Place in a glass bowl and cover with iced water. Let sit for 10 minutes, and drain. Add the sugar, salt and vinegar, remaining spring onion greens and chilli, mixing well.

Place the shredded lettuce on a serving dish and cover with the bean sprouts. Pile the chicken wings on top and serve.

Stir-fried Chicken & Peanuts

Ga xao dau phong

Serves 3–4

2 tablespoons (40 ml/1½ fl oz) peanut oil

400 g (14 oz) chicken breast, sliced

1½ (30 ml/1 fl oz) tablespoons fish sauce

3 spring onions, chopped

1 large mild red chilli, deseeded and sliced

½ cup shelled roasted peanuts

salt and freshly ground black pepper

Heat a wok over high heat and add the oil. Stir-fry the chicken for about 4 minutes, until almost cooked through. Add the fish sauce, spring onions, chilli and peanuts and continue to stir-fry until the chicken and onions are tender, about 1 minute.

Check seasoning, adding salt and pepper to taste.

Chicken Simmered in Coconut Water

Serves 6–8

1 hot red chilli, deseeded and chopped

3 cloves garlic, peeled

2 plump stems lemongrass

6 chicken thighs (preferably with skin on)

6 small chicken drumsticks

2 tablespoons (40 ml/1½ fl oz) oil

2½ tablespoons (50 ml/1¾ fl oz) fish sauce

2-cm (¾-in) piece fresh ginger, peeled

2–3 sprigs fresh green peppercorns (or 1 teaspoon brined peppercorns)

2 × 400-ml (13½-fl oz) cans coconut cream

3 cups cubed winter melon, zucchini or choko

Grind the chili, garlic and 1 stem lemongrass to a paste. Spread over the chicken, add 1 tablespoon (20 ml/¾ fl oz) fish sauce and massage the seasoning into the chicken. Marinate for 20 minutes.

Heat the oil in a large saucepan and brown the chicken a few pieces at a time. Remove to a plate.

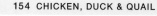

When done, return all the chicken to the saucepan and add the remaining fish sauce, the ginger and peppercorns. Carefully skim off the thick cream from the top of the coconut cream, and use only the clear liquid below. (You can freeze skimmed coconut cream for later use.) Add to the chicken with enough water to not quite cover the chicken and simmer for about 20 minutes. Add the vegetables and continue to simmer, stirring occasionally, until the chicken and vegetables are tender. Check seasonings, and serve.

Stir-fried Chicken, Pineapple & Peppers

Ga xao dua xanh

Serves 4

3 tablespoons (60 ml/2 fl oz) peanut or vegetable oil

5 chicken thigh fillets, cubed

1 small onion, diced

1 red capsicum, diced

3 cloves garlic, chopped

8 small button mushrooms, cut in half

3 spring onions, in 3-cm (1¼ in) pieces

1 hot red chilli, deseeded and chopped

2 tablespoons (40 ml/1½ fl oz) oyster sauce

2 tablespoons (40 ml/1½ fl oz) fish sauce

¾ cup canned or fresh pineapple pieces

salt and freshly ground black pepper

sugar, to taste (optional)

Heat the oil in a wok and stir-fry the chicken on high heat until lightly browned. Remove to a plate using a slotted spoon.

Reheat the wok. Stir-fry onion, capsicum and garlic until softened, about 2 minutes.

Return the chicken and add the mushrooms, onion and chilli and stir-fry for about 2 minutes. Add sauces and 3 tablespoons (60 ml/2 fl oz) water and stir-fry briefly. Stir in the pineapple to warm through. Check seasoning adding salt, pepper and a little sugar if needed, and serve.

Quail with Five-spice Salt & Chilli

Chim quay

Serves 4

1½ tablespoons fine table salt

¾ teaspoon five-spice salt (page 241)

small pinch of chilli powder

4 quails

1 tablespoon (20 ml/¾ fl oz) fish sauce

2 teaspoons dark soy sauce or kecap manis

¾ teaspoon fine white sugar

3 tablespoons (45 g/1½ oz) cornflour

oil for deep frying

2 spring onion greens, chopped

1 large mild red chilli, deseeded and chopped

In a small pan, dry heat the salt for about 1 minute over medium–high heat. Remove from the heat and stir in the five-spice and chilli powders. Tip onto a plate to cool.

Rinse, drain and dry the quail, and cut in half.

Combine the fish sauce, soy sauce, salt and sugar, stirring to dissolve the sugar. Paint over the quail and set aside for 20 minutes to marinate.

Coat the quail lightly and evenly with cornflour.

Heat the oil in a wok fry the quail in two batches over medium–high heat until golden brown and cooked through, about 2 minutes. Drain while the remaining quail are cooked.

Pour off the oil, leaving about 1½ tablespoons (30 ml/1 fl oz). Return the quail with the onion greens, chilli and half of the five-spice salt and toss over high heat until the quail are coated. Serve at once, with the remaining five-spice salt in a small dish for dipping.

Clay Pot Duck with Mushrooms & Bamboo Shoots

Serves 2–4

2 duck legs and thighs

3 tablespoons (60 ml/2 fl oz) peanut or vegetable oil

8 dried black shiitake mushrooms, soaked in hot water for 25 minutes

4 spring onions, in 3-cm (1¼-in) pieces

8 thin slices fresh ginger

2 tablespoons (40 ml/1½ fl oz) oyster sauce

1 tablespoon (20 ml/¾ fl oz) fish sauce

1¼ cups (300 ml/10 fl oz) chicken stock (page 245)

⅓ cup sliced bamboo shoots

3 teaspoons cornflour

Using a Chinese cleaver, chop the duck into 3-cm (1¼-in) pieces, cutting through the bones.

Heat the oil in a wok or saucepan and brown the duck, and then place in a heavy saucepan or clay pot. Add the mushrooms and soaking water strained through a fine sieve. Add the onions, saving some of the greens for garnish, the ginger, sauces and 1 cup (250 ml/8½ fl oz) chicken stock. Bring to the boil, cover tightly and reduce heat to low. Simmer for 40 minutes. Add the bamboo shoots and simmer a further 10 minutes.

Mix cornflour with the remaining chicken stock, pour into the pot and simmer, stirring, over medium–high heat until the sauce thickens. Garnish with the reserved spring onion greens. Serve in the pot.

Roast Duck

Serves 6

1 x 2-kg (4-lb 6-oz) duck

1½ tablespoons Chinese roast
pork seasoning

2 tablespoons (40 ml/1½ fl oz)
dark soy sauce

1 tablespoon (20 ml/¾ fl oz)
fish sauce

1½ tablespoons honey

1½ tablespoons (30 g/1 oz)
soft brown sugar

white rice, to serve

pickled cucumber (page 232),
to serve

Place the duck in a colander in the sink and pour a kettle of boiling water over the skin and into the cavity. Drain well and let dry for a few hours.

In a bowl mix the remaining ingredients with ⅓ cup (80 ml/3 fl oz) boiling water, stirring to dissolve the sugar.

Heat the oven to 180°C (360°F) and set an oven rack over an oven tray in the centre of the oven.

Paint the mixed glaze evenly over the duck and place in the oven to roast for about 1½ hours, brushing with the glaze every 20 minutes. Increase the heat to brown the skin, if required. Serve the duck thinly sliced, with white rice and a side dish of pickled cucumber.

Meat

Vietnam has a thriving cattle industry and beef dishes are star features on restaurant menus, particularly in the central and northern regions where the famed *bo luc lac* (shaking beef) and enterprising celebratory banquet *bo bay mon* (seven styles of beef) are much sought after. At home beef is served mainly on special occasions.

Chinese migrants brought their skills with chopsticks, cleavers and woks to Vietnam, along with a taste for pork, which they sizzle in stir-fries and roast over hot coals. With French know-how, pork pâtés and terrines were introduced into the cuisine, while local cooks made *nems* (meatballs) pounded in stone mortars and simmered in bubbling stock-pots of fresh coconut-water and tangy tamarind.

< Grilled Pork Skewers with Honey Glaze (page 166)

Grilled Pork Skewers with Honey Glaze

Nem nuong

Serves 4

700 g (1 lb 9 oz) pork chops

3 spring onions, white parts only, chopped

3 cloves garlic, peeled

1½ (30 g/1 fl oz) tablespoons sugar

2 tablespoons (40 ml/1½ fl oz) fish sauce

1 tablespoon (20 ml/¾ fl oz) dark soy sauce

3 tablespoons honey

½ teaspoon black pepper

16 bamboo skewers, soaked for 30 minutes

bean-thread noodle salad (page 43)

2–3 tablespoons fried peanuts

sprigs of fresh herbs (dill, mint, coriander, basil)

1 large hot red chilli, deseeded and sliced

Trim fat and bone from pork chops and slice meat thinly. Place in a bowl.

In a spice grinder or mortar, grind the spring onions with garlic and sugar to a paste. Add fish sauce, soy, honey and pepper and mix well. Pour over the pork. Cover and refrigerate for 2 hours, or overnight.

Thread the pork strips onto bamboo skewers and brush lightly with oil. Cook on a hot barbecue or under the grill, turning several times, until slightly charred at the edges and cooked through, about 4 minutes. Brush with any remaining marinade as they cook. Serve over noodle salad garnished with fried peanuts, herbs and chilli.

Roast Pork

Xa xiu

Serves 4–6

1½ tablespoons (30 ml/1 fl oz)
dark soy sauce

1½ tablespoons (30 ml/1 fl oz)
roast pork seasoning

1½ tablespoons (30g/1 oz) soft
brown sugar or honey

2 tablespoons (40 ml/1½ fl oz)
peanut or vegetable oil

400 g (14 oz) pork fillet, fat
and skin trimmed

Preheat the oven to 220°C (390°F). Line an oven tray with baking paper or aluminium foil, and place an oven rack over it.

In a small bowl combine all ingredients except for the pork, stirring to dissolve sugar or honey. Brush thickly over the pork and place on the rack. Roast for about 20 minutes, turning and basting several times with the remaining glaze. Remove from the oven and let sit until cool. Use at once or wrap and refrigerate to use the next day.

 You can purchase pre-sliced Chinese roast pork from Asian grocers.

Pork Meatballs with Lettuce & Herbs

Serves 4–6

500 g (1 lb 2 oz) lean pork, diced

80 g (3 oz) pork fat, diced

2 spring onions, white parts only, diced

6 water chestnuts, drained and very finely diced

1 teaspoon dark soy sauce

3 teaspoons fish sauce

pinch of black pepper

2 tablespoons (40 ml/1½ fl oz) oyster sauce

1 teaspoon hot chilli paste

24 small soft lettuce leaves

24 mint leaves

24 basil leaves or small coriander sprigs

Place the pork in a food processor and grind to a paste. Remove to a bowl.

Put the pork fat and spring onions into the processor and grind smooth. Mix with the pork, adding water chestnuts, soy and fish sauces and a pinch of pepper. Knead and mash the mixture until smooth and slightly sticky.

With oiled hands, shape the mixture into 24 balls and arrange on a plate. Set plate in a steamer over simmering water to cook for about 12 minutes. Remove from the steamer, drain the plate and season meatballs with oyster sauce and chilli paste.

Place the lettuce leaves and herbs on a serving dish with the meatballs. Wrap meatballs and herbs in lettuce just prior to eating.

Spicy Beef in Rice Paper Rolls

Banh uot thit nuong

Serves 4–5

1 stem lemongrass, trimmed and chopped

2 spring onions, whites chopped

1 large clove garlic, peeled

1 small hot red chilli, deseeded

500 g (1 lb 2 oz) rump steak, thinly sliced

1 tablespoon (20 ml/¾ fl oz) fish sauce

2–3 pinches of sugar

2 tablespoons (40 ml/1½ fl oz) vegetable or sesame oil

20 dried rice papers

20 small pieces of lettuce

20 coriander sprigs

20 mint leaves

peanut dipping sauce (page 238)

Place lemongrass, spring onion whites, garlic and chilli in a food processor or blender and grind to a paste. Mix with thinly sliced beef, adding fish sauce and a few small pinches of sugar. Cover and leave for 1 hour.

Heat a wok or frying pan with the oil and stir-fry the beef on very high heat for about 1 minute, until barely cooked. Pile onto a serving plate.

When ready to serve, take a bowl of hot water to the table, along with the rice papers and several clean tea towels. At the table, soften rice papers in the water, drain on tea towels and line with a piece of lettuce, coriander and mint. Add 1–2 beef strips and a small spoonful of the sauce, and roll up. Serve extra sauce for dipping.

Pork Stir-fried with Peanuts & Baby Corn

Serves 4

500 g (1 lb 2 oz) lean pork

3 tablespoons (60 ml/2 fl oz) peanut or vegetable oil

½ cup raw shelled peanuts

2 large cloves garlic, sliced

3 spring onions, sliced into 2-cm (¾-in) pieces

3 thin slices ginger, finely shredded

½ red capsicum, diced

8–10 spears baby corn, halved on an angle

2 tablespoons (40ml/1½ fl oz) fish sauce

3–4 sprigs fresh coriander, roughly chopped

5–6 small mint sprigs, tough stems trimmed

juice of ½ lime or lemon

salt and freshly ground black pepper

Thinly slice the pork and cut into 8-cm (3 in) long strips.

Heat half the oil in a wok over very high heat and stir-fry the pork in two batches, until lightly browned. Remove to a plate.

Reheat wok adding remaining oil and fry the peanuts until lightly golden. Set aside. Add the garlic, onions, ginger and capsicum and stir-fry for about 2½ minutes, until tender. Return pork and the juices from the plate, add corn and peanuts, the fish sauce, herbs, lime or lemon juice and salt and pepper to taste. Stir over high heat for about 30 seconds to mix well.

Pork Terrine

Cha lua

Serves 4–8

3 dried black mushrooms, soaked in hot water for 25 minutes

30 g (1 oz) bean-thread vermicelli, soaked in hot water for 10 minutes

250 g (9 oz) fine pork mince

250 g (9 oz) coarse pork mince

2 cloves garlic, chopped

2 spring onions, white parts only, finely chopped

1 tablespoon (20 ml/¾ fl oz) fish sauce

2 tablespoons (40 ml/1½ fl oz) oyster sauce

1 small hot red chilli, deseeded and finely chopped (optional)

½ teaspoon grated ginger

½ teaspoon black pepper

2 eggs, well beaten

1 banana leaf (optional)

Drain the mushrooms and vermicelli and chop very finely. In a bowl combine all of the ingredients, squeezing through the fingers to achieve a sticky, cohesive mass.

Cut a piece of banana leaf to line a small loaf tin. Brush tin with oil and press leaf into the tin. Fill with the mixture, smoothing the top and brushing it with oil, and cover with another piece of banana leaf. Cover the top of the tin with aluminium foil, pierced in two corners to release excess steam. >

Set the dish in a steamer to steam for about 25 minutes over simmering water. Pierce with a fine skewer and if it comes out dry remove the terrine from the steamer, discard aluminium foil and let rest in the tin for 30 minutes.

Turn out, wrap tightly in cling wrap and refrigerate for at least 3 hours or until firmly set.

Serve with salad, rice or sliced onto a crisp baguette.

Stir-fried Pork & Bean Sprouts

Gia xao thit

Serves 3–4

350 g (12 oz) lean pork, finely shredded

1½ tablespoons (30 ml/1 fl oz) fish sauce

1 teaspoon sugar

1½ teaspoons cornflour

¾ teaspoon black pepper

2 tablespoons (40 ml/1½ fl oz) peanut or vegetable oil

2 teaspoons sesame oil (optional)

4 spring onions, cut into 3-cm (1¼-in) pieces

3 thin slices fresh ginger, cut into fine shreds

250 g (9 oz) fresh bean sprouts

Place shredded pork in a bowl, add the fish sauce, sugar, cornflour and pepper and mix well. Marinate for 15 minutes, stirring occasionally.

Heat the oil in a wok over high heat and add sesame oil (if using). Stir-fry the pork with spring onions and ginger for about 2 minutes, until barely cooked. Add bean sprouts and stir-fry until they wilt, about 1 minute. Check seasoning adding extra fish sauce, if needed.

Sweet & Salty Pork Belly

Thit heo kho tau

Serves 6–8

1 kg (2 lb 3 oz) pork belly or
meaty pork ribs

2 tablespoons (40 ml/1½ fl oz)
peanut or vegetable oil

½ cup (110g/4 oz) caster sugar

½ cup (125 ml/4 fl oz) fish
sauce

1 tablespoon (20 ml/¾ fl oz)
dark soy sauce

4 eggs (optional)

5 spring onions, in 3-cm
(1¼-in) lengths

coriander and vietnamese
mint, for garnish

Cut pork into 3-cm (1¼-in) cubes. Heat the oil in a heavy saucepan over high heat and cook the pork in 2–3 batches until browned. Set aside.

Pour sugar into the pan and cook over high heat, without stirring, until it melts and turns to caramel. Remove from the heat and carefully add the fish and soy sauces, when the bubbling subsides return to the heat and stir to dissolve the caramel toffee. Return the pork and add water to half-cover the meat. Cover the pan and bring to the boil, reduce heat to low and simmer for about 2 hours, turning the meat every 20 minutes.

Meanwhile, boil the eggs (if using) for 9 minutes, cool in cold water, peel and cut in half. Add the spring onions and eggs to the pork, pushing them into the sauce. Simmer gently for 6–7 minutes. Serve garnished with herbs.

Pork Simmered in Coconut Water

Thit nuoc dua

Serves 6

juice of 1 fresh coconut or
  1¾ cups (440 ml/15 fl oz)
  bottled coconut juice

1 kg (1b 2 oz) pork belly or
  boneless leg pork, in 3-cm
  (1¼-in) cubes

½ cup (120 ml/4 fl oz) fish
  sauce

1 stem lemongrass, trimmed
  and chopped

3 cloves garlic, peeled

1 small onion, peeled and
  quartered

2–3 tablespoons (60 ml/2 fl oz)
  peanut or vegetable oil

3 tablespoons golden syrup

1 tablespoon (20 g/¾ oz) soft
  brown sugar

2 star anise

1 teaspoon pepper

Crack open the coconut to extract the juice if using, and set aside.

Season the pork with half the fish sauce and set aside.

In a food processor or spice grinder grind the lemongrass, garlic and onion
to a paste.

Heat the oil in a heavy saucepan and sauté the ground seasoning paste for
about 1 minute. Add the pork and toss to coat with the seasonings. Add the
remaining fish sauce, syrup, sugar, star anise and pepper and stir over high
heat for 1–2 minutes.

Pour in fresh or bottled coconut juice and add water to not quite cover the pork. Bring to the boil, skim any frothy residue which floats to the surface, cover and reduce heat to low. Simmer for 1½–2 hours, until the pork is very tender.

✖ Refreshing coconut water (juice) is sold as a bottled beverage in many Asian grocers. If unobtainable, use coconut milk diluted 50/50 with water.

Grilled Pork Ribs

Suon nuong

Serves 2–4

1 strip pork rib bones, about
10 ribs

1.5-cm (⅝-in) piece fresh
ginger, peeled

2–3 cloves garlic, peeled

1 hot red chilli, deseeded

4–5 sprigs coriander

2 tablespoons (40 ml/1¾ fl oz)
dark soy sauce

1 tablespoon (20 ml/¾ fl oz)
fish sauce

1 tablespoon (15 g/½ oz) sugar

1 tablespoon (20 ml/¾ fl oz) oil

Separate the ribs with a sharp knife and place in a shallow dish.

Place ginger, garlic, chilli and coriander in a food processor or spice grinder and grind to a paste. Mix with soy and fish sauces, sugar and oil and spread over the pork. Cover and marinate for 2 hours (or overnight), turning occasionally.

Heat a charcoal barbecue or hotplate and grill the pork, turning several times, for about 8 minutes, until crisp on the surface and cooked through. Brush with any remaining marinade and extra oil during cooking if needed to keep moist.

Five-spice Butterfly Pork

Serves 4

4 pieces butterfly-cut pork

5-cm (2-in) piece lemongrass, trimmed and chopped

2 cloves garlic, peeled

2 spring onions (white parts only), chopped

1 tablespoon (20 ml/¾ fl oz) fish sauce

¾ teaspoon dark soy sauce

2 teaspoons sugar

¾ teaspoon five-spice powder

pinch of black pepper

2 tablespoons (40 ml/1½ fl oz) peanut or sesame oil

Vietnamese dipping sauce (page 235) or light soy sauce with chopped chilli, for dipping

Place the pork on a cutting board, cover with cling wrap and pound with a meat mallet or rolling pin to make them thin and tender.

In a spice grinder or food processor grind lemongrass, garlic and onion to a paste. Stir in fish and soy sauces, sugar, spices, a pinch of pepper and 1 tablespoon (20 ml/¾ fl oz) peanut or sesame oil. Spread evenly over the pork on both sides, wrap in cling wrap and refrigerate for 2–3 hours (or overnight).

Heat a charcoal barbecue (see note), a hotplate or heavy ribbed pan and rub with paper towel dipped in oil. Brush excess marinade from the pork and brush lightly with oil. Chargrill over high heat for 5–7 minutes until well browned on both sides, turning once or twice.

Leave to rest for a few minutes before cutting into 3-cm (1¼-in) strips. Serve with rice and dipping sauce, or with lettuce and herbs for wrapping.

✳ A camp toaster is an ideal way to cook thin slices of meat (see pages 5–6).

✳ In Vietnam, small pork chops are also cooked like this, the meat pounded flat around the bone.

Shaking Garlic Beef

Bo luc lac

Serves 4

500 g (1 lb 2 oz) rump or
  sirloin steak, diced

1 tablespoon (20 ml/¾ cup)
  fish sauce

1 teaspoon dark soy sauce

5 cloves garlic, chopped

2 spring onions, finely
  chopped

1½ tablespoons (20 g/¾ oz)
  sugar

1 large red onion, sliced

2 teaspoons light soy or fish
  sauce

2 teaspoons rice vinegar

2 teaspoons sugar

80 g (3 oz) small Asian salad
  leaves

2 tablespoons (40 ml/1½ fl oz)
  peanut or vegetable oil

1 large hot red chilli, deseeded
  and thinly sliced (optional)

2 tablespoons (40 ml/1½ fl oz)
  coconut cream (optional)

Marinate the meat in the fish sauce, soy sauce, half the garlic and spring onion, and sugar for 3–4 hours.

Place the onion in a bowl and add soy or fish sauce, vinegar and sugar. Mash with the fingers to separate the strands of onion and soften them. Allow to sit for 10 minutes. Spread the salad leaves on a serving plate.

When the meat is ready to cook heat a wok over very high heat and add the oil. Toss the beef and remaining spring onion and garlic and shake the pan to keep the meat turning until cooked rare to medium-rare. Add chilli and coconut cream (if using), and toss in the very hot wok for a further 30 seconds.

Spread the meat and pan juices over the salad and top with the marinated onions.

Fire-roasted Beef Skewers

Serves 4–5

500 g (1 lb 2 oz) beef rump, sirloin or fillet

2 stem lemongrass, trimmed

2–3 red skinned shallots or 1 small onion, chopped

2 cloves garlic, peeled

1 small hot red chilli, deseeded

2 tablespoons (40 ml/1½ fl oz) fish sauce

2 teaspoons sugar

2 teaspoons dark soy sauce

1 tablespoon (20 ml/¾ fl oz) vegetable oil

bamboo skewers or disposable wooden chopsticks, soaked for 30 minutes

2 tablespoons chopped roasted peanuts

1 small head soft leaf lettuce

½ punnet snow-pea sprouts, or bean sprouts

1 bunch mint, basil or coriander

lime wedges or Vietnamese dipping sauce (page 235)

Cut the beef into thin strips and place in a bowl.

Roughly chop the lemongrass and place in a food processor or spice grinder together with the shallots or onion, garlic and chilli. Grind to a paste, adding the fish sauce, sugar, soy and 2–3 teaspoons of the oil. Spread over the meat, and stir to coat evenly. Cover and marinate for 1 hour.

Prepare a small charcoal barbecue (see page 5), and heat coals until glowing. ❯

Wrap the meat around skewers or chopsticks and roast over high heat for about 3 minutes, turning once or twice, and brushing with any remaining marinade and a little oil.

Squeeze on lime juice, or serve wrapped in lettuce leaves with herbs and sprouts, and Vietnamese dipping sauce.

Fresh Pork Sausage

Cha lua

Serves 4

500 g (1 lb 2 oz) lean pork,
diced

2 tablespoons (40 ml/1½ fl oz)
fish sauce

3 teaspoons rice flour

½ teaspoon sugar

60 g (2 oz) pork fat, very
finely diced

1½ tablespoons (30 ml/1 fl oz)
finely chopped fresh
coriander

1 small hot red chilli, deseeded
and finely chopped (optional)

mustard, chilli sauce or
Vietnamese dipping sauce
(page 235)

Place half the pork in a food processor and grind to a sticky paste. Tip into a bowl. Grind the remaining meat adding fish sauce, rice flour and sugar and add to the first batch. Mix in the pork fat, coriander and chilli (if using), and with wet hands form into 2 sausage shapes.

Wrap each sausage tightly in cling wrap, twisting the ends to keep the roll firm. Refrigerate for 2–3 hours, and then poach in very gently simmering water for about 30 minutes. Remove from the water and set aside to cool. Refrigerate for a further 2 hours, until firm.

Slice and serve cold on toothpicks or in lettuce wraps with mustard, chilli sauce or Vietnamese dipping sauce, for dipping. Or carefully brown in a frying pan or on a hot, oiled grill plate.

Vinegar Beef Steamboat

Bo nhung dam

Serves 4–6

500 g (1 lb 2 oz) beef fillet,
very thinly sliced

freshly ground black pepper

1 large onion, sliced

1 cup (250 ml/8½ fl oz) white
or rice vinegar

3 teaspoons finely chopped
garlic

1 tablespoon (15 g/½ oz) white
sugar

3 tomatoes, deseeded and
diced, or 3 thick slices
pineapple, diced

softened rice papers

strips of lettuce

fresh herbs (mint, coriander,
basil, Vietnamese mint)

shrimp paste dipping sauce
(page 240)

Arrange sliced beef on a platter and season generously with black pepper. Cover and refrigerate. Marinate the sliced onion with 1½ tablespoons (30 ml/1 fl oz) of the vinegar and set aside.

In a saucepan bring 1 L (34 fl oz) water to the boil and add the garlic, sugar and tomatoes or pineapple and remaining vinegar. Reduce heat and simmer for about 15 minutes.

When ready to eat, place a fondue pan or electric frypan on the table. Place the drained marinated onions in a bowl, sliced meat on a plate, the lettuce and herbs on another plate, and prepare a small bowl of the dipping sauce and softened rice papers for each guest.

Strain the vinegar-tomato stock into the pan and heat to a simmer. Using wooden chopsticks, each diner places a slice of meat into the hot stock, retrieving it when barely cooked, to dip into the sauce and wrap with some of the onions, lettuce and a few herb leaves in a softened rice paper.

Vegetables

There's a fresh vegetable market in every Vietnamese village, and, and on every street corner or stretch of country road you'll pass displays of vegetables freshly picked from small farms and rural backyards.

Buddhists maintain a vegetarian code by using soy, and a vegetarian version of oyster sauce, instead of the seafood-based sauces used extensively in Vietnamese kitchens.

Add to this a proliferation of herbs and lettuces, fresh and dried mushrooms, onions, and tofu, and you have the makings of delicious vegetarian food.

‹ Flame-grilled Eggplant Dressed with Spicy Minced Pork (page 196)

Flame-grilled Eggplant Dressed with Spicy Minced Pork

Serves 4

4 slender Asian eggplants

2 tablespoons (40 ml/1½ fl oz) peanut or vegetable oil

3 shallots, finely chopped

1½ tablespoons (30 ml/1 fl oz) finely chopped lemongrass

3 cloves garlic, finely chopped

125 g (4½ oz) pork mince (or chicken mince)

2 tablespoons (40 ml/1½ fl oz) fish sauce

½ teaspoon black pepper

1 small hot red chilli, deseeded and chopped

1½ tablespoons (30 ml/1 fl oz) lime or lemon juice

chopped roasted peanuts

chopped fresh coriander or Vietnamese mint

Place the eggplants directly on a gas flame, in a hot oven, under a medium–hot grill, or over a barbecue, and cook, turning from time to time, until the eggplants are soft and smoky, the skin well-charred.

Transfer to a plastic bag or place in a bowl and cover with cling wrap. Leave for a few minutes while the steam loosens the skin and the eggplants become cool enough to handle and then run under cold water, brushing off the skin. Pat dry with paper towel.

Place side by side on a serving dish and sprinkle with a few teaspoons of the oil.

Heat the remaining oil in a wok and stir-fry shallots, lemongrass and garlic for 30 seconds and then add the pork and stir-fry on high heat until well browned, about 2½ minutes. Season with fish sauce, pepper, chilli and lime or lemon juice.

Spread the pork over the eggplant and garnish with chopped peanuts and the herbs.

Stir-fried Bean Sprouts with Pork & Coriander

Gai xao

Serves 3–4

250 g (9 oz) fresh bean
  sprouts

1½ tablespoons (30 ml/1 fl oz)
  peanut or vegetable oil

1 teaspoon sesame oil

1 clove garlic, finely chopped

3 thin slices fresh ginger, cut
  into fine shreds

100 g (3½ oz) roast pork (page
  167) or sweet and salty pork
  belly (page 178), diced

8–10 small sprigs fresh
  coriander

2 teaspoons light soy sauce

salt

caster sugar, to taste

Blanch the bean sprouts in boiling water for 20 seconds. Drain well and refresh in ice-cold water for 5 minutes. Drain again.

Heat the oils in a wok and stir-fry the bean sprouts with garlic and ginger for about 40 seconds. Add the pork, coriander and soy sauce and season to taste with salt and sugar.

Winter Bamboo Shoots with Mushrooms in Brown Sauce

Mang kho nam huong chay

Serves 4

250 g (9 oz) winter bamboo shoots

8 dried black mushrooms, soaked in boiling water for 25 minutes

1½ tablespoons (30 ml/1 fl oz) vegetable oil

1 tablespoon (20 ml/¾ fl oz) dark soy sauce

2 tablespoons (40 ml/1½ fl oz) light soy sauce

1 tablespoon (20 ml/¾ fl oz) oyster sauce

1½ tablespoons (30 g/1 oz) soft brown sugar

3 small bok choy or tat soi, slit in half

2 teaspoons sesame oil

Drain, rinse and dry the bamboo shoots and cut into 3-cm (1¼-in) chunks. Drain the mushrooms straining the liquid into a bowl and setting it aside.

Heat a wok and add the oil. Stir-fry the bamboo and mushrooms over high heat until the bamboo is lightly browned, about 1½ minutes. Add the soy and oyster sauces and the sugar and stir-fry briefly, and then add about ¾ cup (180 ml/6 fl oz) mushroom water, cover and simmer for about 30 minutes. Add the bok choy or tat soi and simmer for a further 10 minutes. Stir in sesame oil and serve.

✂ Well-stocked Asian food stores sell slender points of winter bamboo shoot in vacuum packs. If not available use canned whole shoots.

Snake Beans with Chicken & Cabbage

Serves 4

1 bunch dark green snake
  beans

6–8 large leaves Chinese
  cabbage

1½ tablespoons (30 ml/1 fl oz)
  peanut or vegetable oil

150 g (5 oz) chicken breast, in
  fine shreds

1 clove garlic, chopped

1 small hot red chilli, deseeded
  and chopped

2 spring onions, finely
  chopped

1½ tablespoons (30 ml/1 fl oz)
  fish sauce

½ teaspoon sugar

Cut the beans into 4-cm (1½-in) pieces. Slice the thick stem ends of the cabbage and roughly chop the crinkly leaves. Heat the oil in a wok and stir-fry the chicken until white and firm, about 45 seconds. Remove to a plate using a slotted spoon.

Add the beans and stir-fry for 30 seconds, and then add the sliced cabbage stems and stir-fry for 30 seconds. Add 1 tablespoon (20 ml/¾ fl oz) water, cover and cook for 40 seconds. Uncover and add the tops of the cabbage leaves and the garlic, chilli and spring onions and stir-fry on high heat for about 40 seconds, until vegetables are crisp and tender. Return the chicken and add the fish sauce and sugar and stir-fry briefly.

Tofu, Beans & Cabbage in Coconut Milk

Hu kho nuoc dua dua

Serves 4

8 large leaves Chinese cabbage

6 snake beans or 18 green beans

1 cup (250 ml/8½ fl oz) peanut or vegetable oil

350 g (12 oz) firm tofu

1 small onion, sliced

1 × 400-ml (13½-fl oz) can coconut milk

2 teaspoons dark soy sauce

2 teaspoons fish sauce

salt

Slice the thick stem ends of the cabbage leaves, and roughly chop the crinkly leaves. Cut beans into 4-cm (1½-in) lengths and bean curd into 2-cm (¾-in) cubes.

Heat the oil in a frying pan or wok and fry the tofu for about 2 minutes, stirring, until lightly browned and crisp on the surface. Remove to a plate.

Pour off all but 1 tablespoon oil (20 ml/¾ fl oz) and stir-fry the onion, beans and stem ends of cabbage for 1 minute. Pour in the coconut milk and add soy and fish sauces and bring to the boil. Return the tofu and add the tender cabbage leaves. Reduce heat and simmer for 8–10 minutes until the vegetables are very tender. Check seasoning adding salt to taste.

Clay Pot Vegetables

Serves 4–6

1 choko, cut into 2-cm (¾-in) cubes

1 large carrot, thickly sliced

1 bunch broccolini, in 4-cm (1½-in) pieces

5 snake beans, in 5-cm (2-in) lengths

1 large zucchini, thickly sliced

3 cloves garlic, chopped

⅓ cup (80 ml/3 fl oz) light soy sauce

1 tablespoon (20 ml/¾ fl oz) dark soy sauce

2½ tablespoons (40 g/1½ oz) sugar

½ teaspoon cracked black pepper

1 cup small button or straw mushrooms, cut in half

300 g (10½ oz) tofu, fried

sesame oil

chopped roasted peanuts and/or chopped herbs

Bring a pot of water to the boil and parboil choko and carrots for 3 minutes. Add broccolini, beans and zucchini and boil for 2 minutes, drain well.

In a clay pot (or heavy saucepan), simmer the soy sauces with sugar and pepper until the sugar has melted. Add the vegetables, garlic, mushrooms and tofu and stir to coat in sauce. Pour in ½ cup water (125 ml/4 fl oz), cover and simmer gently for 5 minutes, stirring occasionally.

Add a little sesame oil, the peanuts, and herbs to garnish. Serve in the pot.

Stir-fried Water Spinach with Garlic & Pepper

Bap su xao tau hu

Serves 3–4

1 large bunch *rau muong*
  water spinach

3 tablespoons (60 ml/2 fl oz)
  peanut or vegetable oil

4 large cloves garlic, finely
  chopped

½ teaspoon black pepper

fish sauce, to taste

Rinse the water spinach and leave the leaves wet. Chop stems into 3-cm (1¼-in) pieces.

Heat the oil in a wok and stir-fry the spinach stems and garlic for about 1 minute. Add the leaves and stir-fry quickly until just wilted. Add pepper and fish sauce to taste, stir-fry quickly, and serve.

Stuffed Tofu in Oyster Sauce

Dau phu nhoi

Serves 4

150 g (5 oz) pork mince

3 dried black mushrooms

2 spring onions, white parts only, finely chopped

1 clove garlic, crushed

½ teaspoon fresh grated ginger

2 teaspoons fish sauce

500 g (1 lb 2 oz) firm tofu

½ cup (75 g) cornflour or tapioca starch

peanut or vegetable oil for deep frying

3 tablespoons (60 ml/2 fl oz) oyster sauce

1 tablespoon (20 ml/¾ fl oz) fish sauce

1½ tablespoons (30 ml/1 fl oz) sugar

Break up the pork in a mixing bowl. Soak mushrooms in hot water for 25 minutes. Drain the mushrooms and chop very finely.

Add mushrooms, onion, garlic, ginger and fish sauce to the pork and squeeze through the fingers until well mixed and sticky.

Cut the tofu into 4-cm (1½-in) squares, and make a deep slit in the centre of each. Gently fill with pork mixture and then coat evenly with cornflour.

Heat oil for deep-frying in a wok and fry the tofu cubes for about 3 minutes, until golden brown and the filling is cooked. Remove and drain on paper towel. ➤

Pour off the oil and in the same wok mix the oyster sauce, fish sauce, sugar and 3 tablespoons (60 ml/2 fl oz) water and bring to a simmer. Return bean curd and stir in the sauce for 1 minute, until well glazed and tender.

Cauliflower with Lemongrass & Basil

Serves 4

1 plump stem lemongrass, trimmed and very finely chopped

1–2 hot red chillies, deseeded and chopped

2 cloves garlic, finely chopped

4 thin slices fresh ginger, cut into fine shreds

¾ teaspoon ground turmeric

2 tablespoons (40 ml/1½ fl oz) light soy or fish sauce

¼ teaspoon black pepper

3 tablespoons (60 ml/2 fl oz) peanut or vegetable oil

½ head cauliflower, separated into small florets

salt

1 bunch small-leaf basil (or Vietnamese mint), leaves picked

In a bowl combine the lemongrass, chillies, garlic, ginger, turmeric, soy or fish sauce and pepper, and set aside.

Heat the oil in a wok and add the cauliflower. Stir-fry over high heat for about 2 minutes, until lightly browned. Add the seasoning mixture and continue to stir-fry until the cauliflower is cooked crisp and tender, about 2 minutes. Check seasoning adding salt to taste, and fold in the basil or mint.

Fried Tofu in Spicy Tomato Sauce

Dau phu sot ca chua

Serves 3–4

1 cup (250 ml/8½ fl oz) peanut or vegetable oil

400 g (14 oz) firm tofu, cut into 2-cm cubes

1 medium-sized onion, finely sliced

1–2 hot red chillies, deseeded and sliced

4 thin slices fresh ginger, cut into fine shreds

1 × 410-g (14-oz) can crushed tomatoes

2 tablespoons (40 ml/1½ fl oz) fish sauce

1 teaspoon cracked black pepper

½ teaspoon sugar

2–3 tablespoons finely shredded Vietnamese mint or coriander

2 tablespoons crisp-fried onions or garlic (page 230)

Heat the oil in a wok and fry the tofu until golden brown, about 2 minutes. Remove to a strainer to drain. Pour off all but 1 tablespoon (20 ml/¾ fl oz) of the oil and fry the onion, chillies and ginger for 2 minutes, until onion is browned. Add crushed tomatoes, fish sauce, pepper and sugar and simmer for about 7 minutes, adding a few spoonfuls water if it is very thick. Fold in the tofu and most of the herbs and simmer gently for 1–2 minutes.

Garnish with the remaining herbs, and the crisp-fried onions or garlic.

Sweets

Sweet dishes and fruit drinks are enjoyed throughout the day in Vietnam. Tropical fruit, locally grown spices, dried beans and nuts, plain and glutinous (sticky) rice, sugarcane and even vegetables are converted into an array of sweet desserts, snacks, puddings and refreshing beverages – some as simple as sliced fresh fruit sprinkled with salt and chilli powder.

Desserts are garnished with fruit, crunchy roast peanuts, cashew nuts or sesame seeds, and sprigs of mint or sticks of lemongrass. French classics such as crème brûlée, as well as savoury and sweet breads also feature prominently.

< Cardamom Crème Brûlée (page 214)

Cardamom Crème Brûlée

Serves 4–6

1¾ cups (450 ml/15 fl oz)
  cream
6 cardamom pods, cracked
1 split vanilla bean
6 egg yolks
⅓ cup (75 g/2⅔ oz) fine white
  sugar, plus extra

Preheat the oven to 170°C (340°F).

Combine the cream, cardamom and vanilla bean in a saucepan and bring barely to the boil, reduce heat and simmer gently for about 6 minutes. Remove from the heat and let stand for a further 5 minutes.

Whisk the egg yolks with sugar in a bowl until light and creamy. Strain in the heated cream, discarding the spices. Divide between 4–6 ramekins and set in an oven dish. Add enough warm water to come halfway up the sides of the ramekins and cook for around 30 minutes, until custard sets.

Let cool and refrigerate until quite cold. Spread fine sugar over the surface and glaze with a little kitchen torch, or set the dishes in a pan of cold water and place under a very hot grill just long enough for the sugar to caramelise.

Caramel Pineapple Sticks

Serves 6–8

1 small fresh pineapple

6–8 bamboo skewers, soaked
  for 20 minutes

1 cup (220 g/8 oz) sugar

1 vanilla bean, split lengthways

1 cinnamon stick

4 cloves

8 large mint leaves, finely
  shredded

Peel the pineapple and cut out any dark eyes. Cut lengthways into wedges and trim off the tough core from each wedge. Push a bamboo skewer into each piece of pineapple.

Place the sugar in a large, shallow pan and cook over medium heat without stirring until it begins to caramelise, shaking the pan occasionally. Remove from the heat and add ⅓ cup (80 ml/3 fl oz) water, taking care as it bubbles and splutters. Return to the heat and simmer gently, stirring, until any lumps of toffee have melted back into the syrup. Add the pineapple sticks and spices and gently simmer, turning frequently, until the pineapple pieces are glazed with the syrup.

Scatter mint leaves over and serve hot.

Lime Sago with Fruit

Serves 6

**1 cup sago or tapioca, soaked
for 25 minutes**

1⅓ cup (295g/10⅔ oz) sugar

zest and juice of 3 limes

**red papaya, rambutans,
starfruit or tamarillo, sliced**

Place drained sago or tapioca, ⅓ cup (75 g/2⅔ oz) sugar and lime juice and zest in a saucepan with 3 cups (750 ml/25 fl oz) water and bring to the boil, stirring. Reduce heat and simmer, stirring frequently, until thick, about 15 minutes.

Rinse out small dessert moulds or a larger mould or round bowl with cold water and fill with the sago or tapioca. Cover, cool and refrigerate until set (at least 1 hour).

In a small saucepan over medium heat, stir remaining sugar into 1 cup (250ml/8½ fl oz) water until all sugar is dissolved. Gently bring to the boil, then remove from heat and set aside to cool.

Turn out moulds onto dessert plates or a larger serving plate. Surround with the sliced fruit and drizzle with syrup.

Cinnamon Fried Bananas

Serves 4

1 cup (150 g/5 oz) plain flour

1 teaspoon baking powder

⅓ teaspoon salt

4 ladies' finger bananas

⅓ cup (50 g/1¾ oz) cornflour
  or tapioca starch

oil for deep-frying

⅓ cup (75 g/2½ oz) fine white
  sugar

1½ teaspoons ground
  cinnamon

thick cream, coconut cream or
  ice-cream, to serve (optional)

Mix the flour, baking powder and salt in a bowl, and then stir in enough water to make a batter that is slightly thick and creamy. Let rest for 20 minutes.

Peel the bananas and slice lengthways into thin slices. Dust with cornflour or tapioca starch.

Check the batter with a piece of banana. If too thick add a few spoonfuls of water. Heat enough oil for deep-frying. Coat the banana slices one at a time, sliding them immediately into the oil to fry over medium–high heat until golden brown and crisp. Drain on paper towel.

Mix the sugar and cinnamon together and sprinkle over the bananas while still warm. Serve with thick cream, coconut cream or ice-cream if desired.

Bananas in Coconut Cream

Che chuoi

Serves 3–4

3 large ripe bananas

1 × 400-ml (13½-fl oz)
  can coconut cream

1 vanilla bean, split
  lengthways

sugar, to taste

salt

Peel the bananas and cut at an angle into 3-cm (1¼-in) pieces.

Pour coconut cream into a saucepan. Add 1½ cups (375 ml/12½ fl oz) water, the vanilla bean and about 3 tablespoons (45 g/1¾ oz) sugar. Bring to the boil, reduce heat and simmer for 2 minutes.

Add the pieces of banana and a pinch of salt and simmer gently for about 6 minutes.

Serve warm or cold.

Silken Tofu in Syrup

Dau hu duong

Serves 4

500 g (1 lb 2 oz) silken (soft) tofu

2 stems lemongrass or 2 × 12-cm (5-in) stems sugarcane

¾ cup (170 g/6 oz) white sugar

mint leaves (optional), finely shredded

Carefully cut the tofu into bite-sized pieces, place in a bowl, and cover with ice-cold water and set aside.

Trim lemongrass and cut into 8-cm (3-in) pieces. Split lemongrass or sugarcane lengthways and bat with a heavy knife or cleaver to bruise and release flavours.

Simmer sugar, lemongrass or sugarcane in 1½ cups (375 ml/12½ fl oz) water for about 12 minutes, stirring occasionally. Discard lemongrass or sugarcane.

Drain the tofu and pour on the hot sauce. Serve at once, or chill and serve garnished with mint leaves.

Banana Rice Pudding

Serves 2–3

2 cups cooked rice

1 × 400-ml (13½-fl oz) can coconut cream

2 tablespoons (25 g/⅞ oz) soft brown or grated palm sugar

2 tablespoons chopped cashew nuts

2 ripe bananas, diced

Combine rice, coconut cream, sugar and cashew nuts in a saucepan and bring to the boil.

Reduce heat and simmer gently for about 8 minutes until rice has absorbed much of the coconut cream. Add the bananas and cook gently for 2 minutes. Serve warm or cold.

White Corn in Sweet Soup

Serves 4–6

3 cobs fresh white corn or
¾ cup dried white corn
kernels

½ cup split yellow mung beans

1 × 400-ml (13½-fl oz) can
coconut cream

½ stem lemongrass, split
lengthways

½ cup (110 g/4 oz) sugar

⅓ teaspoon salt

1 tablespoon (15g/½ oz)
cornflour (optional)

If using fresh corn, cut off the kernels with a sharp knife, working over a plate to save the juices. If using dried corn, soak overnight, drain and steam for about 20 minutes until almost tender.

Transfer fresh or steamed corn to a saucepan and add the remaining ingredients and 2 cups (500 ml/17 fl oz) water. Bring to the boil, reduce heat and simmer for about 20 minutes, or until the rice and mung beans are completely soft and breaking up.

The soup should be reasonably thick. If not, stir cornflour into 3 tablespoons cold water and add to the soup. Stir and simmer for 3–4 minutes. Serve warm or cold.

Rainbow Coconut Drink

Che

Serves 2

1 cup (220 g/8 oz) caster sugar

1 cup crushed ice

1 cup (250 ml/8½ fl oz) coconut milk

¾ cup (180 ml/6 fl oz) any of the following: pea-sized balls of melon or papaya; cooked rainbow-coloured tapioca or sago; little cubes of chewy jelly made with agar agar, sweetened water and food colouring

In a small saucepan over medium heat, stir sugar into 1 cup (250 ml/8½ fl oz) water until sugar is dissolved. Remove from heat and allow to cool. Syrup can be made ahead of time and kept in a refrigerator for up to a month.

Over crushed ice half-fill tall glasses with coconut milk and sweeten to taste with sugar syrup. Divide remaining ingredients between glasses and serve.

Iced drinks known as 'rainbow' or 'bubble drink' are popular snacks in Vietnam. The ingredients they use are a surprising combination of fruit, dessert ingredients and cooked vegetables. The drinks are traditionally served with a long handled spoon, often replaced with a large plastic straw.

Extras

Pickled shallots, carrots, garlic and baby leeks, which are sold in cans and jars at Vietnamese stores and markets, accompany many Vietnamese meals, even soups.

Salty, sweet, fresh and tangy are the taste elements in Vietnamese dipping sauces and salad dressings. They are easy to make and are essential accompaniments to many dishes.

< Pickled Carrot & Daikon (page 228)

Pickled Carrot & Daikon

Makes 2 cups

1 large carrot

23-cm (9-in) piece daikon

½ cup (125ml/4 fl oz) rice vinegar

1¼ tablespoons (20g/¾ oz) sugar

½ teaspoon salt

Peel the carrot and daikon and cut into 5-cm (2-in) lengths. With a sharp knife slice the carrot and daikon pieces thinly, and then stack 3–4 slices together and cut into fine shreds. Place in a heatproof bowl.

Meanwhile in a small saucepan combine the vinegar, sugar and salt with ⅔ cup (160 ml/5½ fl oz) water and bring to the boil. Simmer for 30 seconds and remove from the heat. Pour over the carrots and daikon, stir and cover. Let marinate for at least 1 hour before using.

Store in a clean jar in the refrigerator where it will keep for up to 2 weeks.

Marinated Bean Sprouts

Makes 1 cup

**250 g (9 oz) fresh bean
  sprouts**

**3 tablespoons (60 ml/2 fl oz)
  rice vinegar**

**2 tablespoons (30 g/1 oz) fine
  white sugar**

2 teaspoons salt

Place bean sprouts in a bowl and cover with boiling water. Let sit for 2–3 minutes, and then drain. Mix together the vinegar, sugar and salt and pour over the bean sprouts, mixing well. Cover and set aside for 1–2 hours, stirring occasionally. Drain thoroughly to use.

✕ Fresh-pickled bean sprouts make a refreshing side dish, however they must be used on the day they are made.

Crisp-fried Onions

Makes ⅓ cup

10 shallots, sliced

3 small onions or 2 baby leeks, sliced

vegetable or peanut oil for frying

Heat oil in a wok to medium hot. Add the finely sliced small red or brown skinned shallots, small onions or baby leeks and fry in vegetable or peanut oil over medium heat until they are crisp and dry and a deep golden brown. Take care they are not overcooked which will make them bitter. Lift out and drain on paper towel.

✂ You can use the same method for crisp-fried garlic.

✂ A crunchy garnish for soup, noodles, rice dishes and grills. When cold and crisp, they can be stored in an airtight container for a couple of weeks, for convenient use.

Spring Onion Oil

Makes ⅓ cup

¾ cup (180 ml/6 fl oz) peanut
  or vegetable oil

1 bunch spring onions, finely
  chopped

Heat the oil in a small saucepan and add spring onion. Cook for about 3 minutes over medium heat, stirring constantly. Strain and return a few teaspoons of the cooked spring onions to the oil.

Keep refrigerated for up to 2 weeks.

Pickled Cucumber

Makes 1 cup

2 small cucumbers

⅓ cup (80 ml/3 fl oz) rice vinegar

1½ tablespoons (25 g/⅞ oz) sugar

½ teaspoon salt

2 shallots, finely sliced

2 fresh red chillies, deseeded and sliced

Cut unpeeled cucumbers lengthways in half and scoop out the seeds. Slice thinly.

In a bowl mix the vinegar, sugar and salt with 2 tablespoons (40 ml/1½ fl oz) water, stirring to dissolve sugar. Add the cucumber, shallots and chilli, mix well cover and set aside for at least 40 minutes, turning occasionally.

Pickled cucumber will keep in the refrigerator for about 10 days.

Vietnamese Dipping Sauce

Nuoc cham

Makes about 1½ cups

3 tablespoons (60 ml/2 fl oz)
  lemon juice

3 tablespoons (60 ml/2 fl oz)
  sugar syrup

¾ cup cold water

½ teaspoon finely chopped
  chilli

1 teaspoon finely crushed
  garlic

3 tablespoons (60 ml/2 fl oz)
  fish sauce

Whisk all the ingredients together. Use immediately or keep in a sterilised jar in the refrigerator for up to 5 days.

Caramel Sauce

Makes ⅔ cup

½ cup (110 g/4 oz) sugar

⅓ cup (80 ml/3 fl oz) fish sauce

2 red skinned shallots, thinly
  sliced (optional)

freshly ground black pepper
  (optional)

Heat the sugar in a saucepan over low–medium heat until it melts and turns to caramel. Remove from the heat and add fish sauce, taking care as it will bubble up and splatter. The sugar will harden into a lump. Return to the stove to heat gently over low heat until it melts again. Add the shallots and pepper, if using, and let cool.

To keep for more than 3–4 days in the refrigerator, leave out the shallots.

Chilli & Lime Dipping Sauce

Nuoc mam chanh

Makes ¾ cup

1 clove garlic, finely chopped

1 small hot red chilli, finely chopped

3 tablespoons (60 ml/2 fl oz) lime juice

2½ tablespoons (50 ml/1¾ fl oz) fish sauce

2 tablespoons (40 ml/1½ fl oz) water

pinch of sugar (optional)

1–2 tablespoons spring onions greens or garlic chives, finely chopped (optional)

Mix the ingredients together, taste for a balance of salty, hot and sour. Add a pinch of sugar if you like. This dipping sauce will keep for 1–2 days in the refrigerator, longer without spring onion or chives.

Finely shredded kaffir lime leaf, coriander or ginger can be added, to taste.

Peanut Dipping Sauce

Nuoc leo

Makes 2 cups

2 cloves garlic, chopped

2 hot red chillies, deseeded
and chopped

½ cup (140 g/5 oz) crunchy
peanut butter

1 cup (250 ml/8½ fl oz)
chicken stock (page 245)
or water

¼ cup (60ml/2 fl oz)
coconut milk

1 tablespoon (20 ml/¾ fl oz)
fish sauce

2 tablespoons (40 ml/1½ fl oz)
hoisin sauce

1 tablespoon (15 g/½ oz) sugar

Combine all ingredients and mix well.

Use immediately or refrigerate in a sterilised jar for up to 1 week.

Shrimp Paste Dipping Sauce

Mam tom

Makes about ⅓ cup

1 small clove garlic, finely
chopped

1 small hot red chilli, deseeded
and chopped

1 tablespoon shrimp paste

1 tablespoon (15 g/½ oz) sugar

3 tablespoons (60 ml/2 fl oz)
lemon or lime juice

1½ tablespoons (30 ml/1 fl oz)
fish sauce

Combine the ingredients, mixing well and adding fish sauce to make a
salty, pungent sauce with a hint of sweetness.

This dipping sauce will keep in a sterilised jar in the refrigerator for 4–5 days.

✶ 4 tablespoons (80ml/3 fl oz) pineapple juice can replace sugar and
citrus juice. Thin with a little cold water if needed.

Five-spice Salt

Huong liu muoi

Makes 1¾ tablespoons

1½ tablespoons fine table salt

1½ teaspoons five-spice
powder

In a dry pan heat the salt for about 40 seconds and add the five-spice powder. Stir a few times, and then remove to a plate to cool.

Salad Dressing

Makes ¾ cup

2 cloves garlic, finely chopped

1 medium-sized hot red chilli,
deseeded and chopped

3 tablespoons (60 ml/2 fl oz)
lime juice

3 tablespoons (60 ml/2 fl oz)
fish sauce

2 tablespoons (40 ml/1½ fl oz)
fine white sugar, or to taste

Mix the ingredients together, whisking to dissolve sugar. Adjust with extra lime, fish sauce or sugar to suit your taste.

Use this dressing on your favourite Vietnamese salad.

Fish Stock

Makes about 5 cups

**1 kg (2 lb 3 oz) fish heads and
frames**

1 small onion, quartered

1 stick celery, chopped

**1 fresh fennel stem, chopped,
or ⅓ teaspoon lightly
crushed fennel seeds**

2 peppercorns

Rinse and drain the heads and frames and place in a large saucepan with the onion, celery, fennel stem or seeds and peppercorns.

Add 5–6 cups (about 1.5 L/3 pt 3 fl oz) of water and slowly bring to the boil.

Reduce heat to low and simmer gently for no more than 20 minutes.

Strain and freeze if not using at once.

Fresh fish stock is hard to beat for taste. Most cubes and powders do not quite capture the subtle flavour of fish and almost always contain too much salt. You can buy fish 'frames', the comb-like backbone, and whole heads from any fishmonger.

Chicken Stock

Makes about 1.5 L (3 pt 3 fl oz)

1 kg (2 lb 3 oz) chicken bones
   or wings
500 g (1 lb 2 oz) chicken necks
1 small onion, cut in half
2-cm (¾-in) piece fresh ginger,
   cut in two

Place chicken bones or wings and necks in a large saucepan and cover with cold water. Let sit for 5 minutes, and then drain.

Cover again with at least 2 L (4 pt 4 fl oz) water. Add the onion and ginger and bring to the boil. Reduce heat to a slow simmer and carefully skim the surface for froth and impurities. Simmer for about 20 minutes, skimming as needed, and then strain into a clean saucepan or containers for freezing.

This stock can be refrigerated for no more than 2 days, or frozen for up to 4 months.

Rich Beef Stock

Makes about 2 L (4 pt 4 fl oz)

4 kg (8 lb 14 oz) beef stock bones

1 kg (2 lb 3 oz) beef ribs

2 onions

10 cloves

6 small shallots, unpeeled

4-cm (1½-in) piece fresh galangal (or ginger), unpeeled

1 plump stem lemongrass, bruised

10-cm (4-in) piece daikon

6 star anise

2 cinnamon sticks

Soak bones in cold water overnight, and drain well. Spread in an oven dish.

Preheat oven to 200°C (400°F).

Peel the onions and stud with the cloves (push them into the onion). Place in the oven dish. Cook for about 30 minutes in a hot oven, turning once. Transfer to a large stock pot and add water to generously cover. Bring to the boil and skim off the froth and impurities which float to the surface.

Reduce heat, add shallots, galangal, lemongrass and daikon, the star anise and cinnamon and simmer for about 5 hours, skimming as necessary and topping up with water if it is boiling away too fast.

Strain stock through a sieve lined with clean cloth. Use at once, refrigerate for no more than 2 days, or freeze for up to 4 months.

Special Ingredients

BASIL Most types can be used – Greek, holy, purple, opal, etc. Good in herb gardens and pots.

BEAN SPROUTS Keep for only a few days in the fridge. Blanch in boiling water, drain and refresh in iced water to use.

BEAN-THREAD VERMICELLI Firm transparent noodles made from vegetable or mung starch. They are sold dried and must be soaked before use.

BETEL LEAVES Fresh and pickled *bo la lot* or betel leaves (also sold under their Thai name *bai champlu*) are a heart-shaped leaf with a pleasantly spicy flavour.

CANNED CRAB This is sold in well-stocked Asian stores. Minced crab with spices is often labelled '*gia vi cua nau bun rieu*'.

CHILLIES Use longer varieties of red and green chillies, which are medium to hot in taste. Bottled crushed hot red chilli is a good standby ingredient.

CHINESE SPRING-ROLL WRAPPERS These are easy to use as they do not need to be soaked, and the rolls are cooked in hot oil for only about 2½ minutes.

CORIANDER (Chinese parsley/cilantro) It can be difficult to grow at home, but sold in most supermarkets and Asian food shops. Coriander keeps for a few days if wrapped in paper towel and refrigerated. Saw Leaf Coriander has 8 cm flat leaves with serrated edges. Good alternative to fresh coriander, and grows well in a herb garden.

FISH SAUCE (*Nuoc mam*) This salty amber-coloured, fermented fish sauce is used in almost everything, and can be replaced with light soy sauce if necessary.

GARLIC AND GARLIC CHIVES Buy firm, pink tinged bulbs of fresh garlic. Garlic chives and flowering garlic chives are sold in Asian stores and most supermarkets. Keep in the vegetable crisper, wrapped in paper towel.

GINGER Pale-skinned young ginger is best. Slice, shred, chop, grate, use in chunks. Plastic squeeze bottles and jars of crushed ginger are good refrigerator basics.

INSTANT VIETNAMESE SOUR SOUP (*Rau om va gia vi nau canh chua*) Bottled stock paste for tangy soup stocks (tamarind or pineapple based). Use about 1 teaspoon of paste to 1 cup of water, adjusting to taste.

LIMES Smooth skinned standard variety. Keep a bottle of lime juice in the fridge for when fresh limes are too expensive or not available.

LEMONGRASS This stem herb keeps for several weeks in the fridge. The lower 15 cm (6 in) is used, in chunks, slit in half, or very finely sliced. Readily available. Chopped ready to use lemongrass can be used in sauces and seasoning pastes.

MUSHROOMS Asian mushrooms (shiitake, enoki, wood fungus, etc) are sold fresh by the punnet. Plan to use them within 2–3 days of buying to ensure freshness. Small fresh button mushrooms can replace canned straw mushrooms in any recipe.

NOODLES Fresh rice sheets/noodles keep for 2–4 days after purchase. Do not overcook or they will fill apart. Use straight from pack, or if oily rinse quickly with hot water.

SHRIMP PASTE (*Mam tom* or *man ruoc*) A pungent shrimp paste used in sauces and in a strongly flavoured dipping sauce also called *mam tom*. A simple combination of light soy sauce and sliced chilli goes with vegetarian dishes.

STOCK PASTE (*Gia vi nau pho*) Bottled stock paste for *pho* and other beef soups.

TAMARIND PASTE This can be purchased concentrated (ready to use), in jars. Refrigerate after opening.

TARO A tuber vegetable that can be prepared in the same way as potato. The leaves can be cooked in the same way as spinach. Available from Asian grocers.

TOFU Use soft beancurd for soups and firm when stir-frying, braising and deep frying. Keeps for a couple of days in the fridge after opening.

VIETNAMESE MINT A peppery, narrow-leafed herb, commonly used in Vietnamese cooking.

WATER SPINACH (*Rau muong*) A spinach-like vegetable. Spinach and watercress are suitable substitutes.

Conversions

Important note: All cup and spoon measures given in this book are based on Australian standards. The most important thing to remember is that an Australian cup = 250 ml, while an American cup = 237 ml and a British cup = 284 ml. Also, an Australian tablespoon is equivalent to 4 teaspoons, not 3 teaspoons as in the United States and Britain. US equivalents have been provided throughout for all liquid cup/spoon measures. Equivalents for dry ingredients measured in cups/spoons have been included for flour, sugar and rising agents such as baking powder. For other dry ingredients (chopped vegetables, nuts, etc.), American cooks should be generous with their cup measures – slight variations in quantities of such ingredients are unlikely to affect results.

VOLUME

Australian cups/spoons	Millilitres	US fluid ounces
* 1 teaspoon	5 ml	
1 tablespoon (4 teaspoons)	20 ml	¾ fl oz
1½ tablespoons	30 ml	1 fl oz
2 tablespoons	40 ml	1½ fl oz
¼ cup	60 ml	2 fl oz
⅓ cup	80 ml	3 fl oz
½ cup	125 ml	4 fl oz
¾ cup	180 ml	6 fl oz
1 cup	250 ml	8½ fl oz
4 cups	1 L	34 fl oz

*the volume of a teaspoon is the same around the world

SIZE

Centimetres	Inches
1 cm	⅜ in
2 cm	¾ in
2.5 cm	1 in
5 cm	2 in
10 cm	4 in
15 cm	6 in
20 cm	8 in
30 cm	12 in

TEMPERATURE

Celsius	Fahrenheit
150°C	300°F
160°C	320°F
170°C	340°F
180°C	360°F
190°C	375°F
200°C	390°F
210°C	410°F
220°C	420°F

WEIGHT

Grams	Ounces
15 g	½ oz
30 g	1 oz
60 g	2 oz
85 g	3 oz
110 g	4 oz
140 g	5 oz
170 g	6 oz
200 g	7 oz
225 g	8 oz (½ lb)
450 g	16 oz (1 lb)
500 g	1 lb 2 oz
900 g	2 lb
1 kg	2 lb 3 oz

Index

LONDON, NEW YORK, MUNICH,
MELBOURNE AND DELHI

First published in Great Britain in 2011 by
Dorling Kindersley, 80 Strand, London, WC2R 0RL

A Penguin Company

Published by Penguin Group (Australia), 2010
250 Camberwell Road, Camberwell, Victoria 3124, Australia
(a division of Pearson Australia Group Pty Ltd)

10 9 8 7 6 5 4 3 2 1

Design by Marley Flory © Penguin Group (Australia)
Photography by Julie Renouf
Food styling by Lee Blaylock
Typeset in Nimbus Sans Novus by Post Pre-press Group, Brisbane, Queensland
Scanning and separations by Splitting Image P/L, Clayton, Victoria
Printed and bound in China by Everbest Printing Co. Ltd

A CIP catalogue record for this book is available from the British Library.

ISBN: 978-1-4053-6419-5

Discover more at www.dk.com